Citizenship Studies

for AQA GCSE Short Course

FOUNDATION EDITION

Citizenship Studies

for AQA GCSE Short Course

FOUNDATION EDITION

Cathy Rushforth

Hodder & Stoughton

A MEMBER OF THE HODDER HEADLINE GROUP

Dedicated to Lindsay and Alex, in the hope that their generation gain from their study of Citizenship.

Acknowledgements

The publishers would like to thank the following individuals, institutions and companies for permission to reproduce copyright illustrations in this book:

AP Photos: p112 (tl) Achmad Ibrahim, (r) Moshe Bursuker, p91 (t) Ruth Fremson; p13 Jacqueline Burden; BBC Picture Archives: p72; ChildLine: p72; Neil Cooper Pictures: p75; Corbis: p7 Raymond Gehman, pp8, 88 Bettman/Corbis, p92 Francoise de Mulder; p12 Richard T Nowitz, p81 (l) Chris Rainier; p14 Roger Ressmeyer, p16 Flip Schulke, p20 Robert & Linda Mostyn/Eye Ubiquitous, p24 (t) Ian Harwood/Ecoscene, (m) Owen Franken, (b) Robert Holmes, p26 (b) Nik Wheeler, p28 (r) So Hing-Keung, p44 (m) Najlah Feanny, p44 (2r) Craig Aurness, pp46 (r), p83 David Turnley, p55 John Heseltine, p81 Robert Holmes, p101 Vittoriano Rastelli, pp103, 106(b) Peter Johnson, p104 Robert Maass, p106 (t)Owen Franken, p108 Joe Bator, p112 (bl) Michael S Yamashita; Council of Europe: pp 44 (l), 56; Express Newspapers p67 (mr); Melanie Friend/Format/Photofusion: p96 (b); Foto Web UPPA Ltd/Topham: p70 (r); Café Direct: p95 (l); Hulton Archive: p86 Hulton Getty/Fox Photos; ITN: p72 (br); Life File: p38 (l) Mike Evans; Mirrorpix: p67 (ml); PA News: p38 (r) Martin Keane; News International Syndication: p67 (far tl); PA Photos: pp39, 60 (l); pp9, 42 (m), 44 (r), 67 (b), 80, 91 (b), 97, 100, 101, 126 EPA, p26 (t) Owen Humphreys, p28 (l) Sean Dempsey, p33 David Cheskin, p40, p44 (2l) Fiona Hanson, p42 Barry Batchelor, p51 Phil Noble, p60 (r) Matthew Fearn, pp61, 72(t) John Giles, p63 Justin Williams, p65 Peter Jordan, p42 (r), pp 42 (r), 68 (t) Toby Melville, p71 Yui Mok, p98 (t) Andy Butterton; Photodisk: p22; Photofusion: p6 David Tothill, p11 Gina Glover, p15 G Montgomery, pp29, 32 Paul Doyle, pp30, p46 (l) Brian Mitchell, p34 (t) Peter Olive, p34 (b) Don Gray, p48 Ute Klaphake, p77 Mark Campbell, p95 (r) Paul Bigland, p109; Reuters: p67 (tr); Rex Features Ltd: p31 Ray Tang, pp37 (t), 73 Nils Jorgensen, p57 Tony Kyriacou, p70 (l) Dan Herrick, p88 (l) Sipa Press; Ronald Grant Archive: p72; Shelter: p37 (b); Photo reproduced by kind permission of Doreen Lawrence, Director of the Stephen Lawrence Trust: p62; Still Pictures: pp96(t), 98 (r) Hartmut Schwarzbach; The Sun: p69; Topham/Picturepoint: p105.

The publishers would also like to thank the following for permission to reproduce material in this book:

A message from the HM Queen Elizabeth , 11 March 2002: p28 reproduced with the permission of the Controller of HMSO and the Queen's printer for Scotland; Oxfam Community Aid Abroad: p97.

Every effort has been made to trace and acknowledge ownership of copyright. The publishers will be glad to make suitable arrangements with any copyright holders whom it has not been possible to contact.

Note about the Internet links in the book. The user should be aware that URLs or web addresses change regularly. Every effort has been made to ensure the accuracy of the URLs provided in this book on going to press. It is inevitable, however, that some will change. It is sometimes possible to find a relocated web page, by just typing in the address of the home page for a website in the URL window of your browser.

Orders: please contact Bookpoint Ltd, 130 Milton Park, Abingdon, Oxon OX14 4SB. Telephone: (44) 01235 827720. Fax: (44) 01235 400454. Lines are open from 9.00–6.00, Monday to Saturday, with a 24 hour message answering service. You can also order through our website www.hodderheadline.co.uk.

British Library Cataloguing in Publication Data
A catalogue record for this title is available from the British Library

ISBN 0 340 81306 7

First Published 2004
Impression number   10 9 8 7 6 5 4 3 2 1
Year   2008 2007 2006 2005 2004

Copyright © 2004 Cathy Rushforth

Cover photo from Digital Vision.
Typeset by Pantek Arts Ltd, Maidstone, Kent.
Colour reproductions by Dot Gradations Ltd, UK.
Printed in Italy for Hodder & Stoughton Educational, a division of Hodder Headline, 338 Euston Road, London NW1 3BH.

Contents

Introduction

KEY ISSUES

○ **What makes someone a good citizen?**
○ **How can we make the right choices?**
○ **How might our choices affect other people?**

Choices and Decisions

It's not what you know, it's what you do with the knowledge that counts.

Citizenship lessons aim to help you understand how society works. This will give you the skills to be an active citizen in a democracy.

Citizenship is about:

- fairness
- democracy
- justice
- rights
- responsibilities
- participation
- choice

This book looks at how citizenship is developed through:

1 School, Work and the Local Community
2 National and European Citizenship
3 Global Citizenship

Citizens need to:

1 find out the facts
2 consider different options
3 weigh up what the results of different actions would be
4 make a decision
5 take action
6 learn from mistakes and successes
7 decide how to actively campaign for a fairer society.

But deciding what is the right choice or decision to make is not always easy. Trying to work out what is the best course of action can be hard.

How Can You Decide What is Right and What is Wrong?

You can't just consider yourself. You need to think about:

- What effect your actions will have on others
- Is it allowed/is it against the law?
- Is it morally right? Does it fit my religious beliefs?
- What would my parents and peers (friends) think?

Shane needs new trainers for school. Is this just a personal decision?

Sort out which of these issues are personal and which involve citizenship issues.

- What size?
- What colour?
- What make?
- Can I/my parents afford them?
- Do I need to look cool and buy a brand my classmates would approve of?
- Were the workers who made the brand exploited?
- Is the company **eco-friendly**?
- Would cheap trainers be a genuine bargain or fall apart?
- Would expensive trainers actually last any longer/be more comfortable?

Shane knows that most of his friends wear a particular brand of trainers. They are seen as cool. But he has heard that the company that produces them has a bad reputation. People say:

- they use child labour
- they don't protect their employees' safety
- wages are so low that workers have to work 16 hours a day to earn enough to live on
- there is no sick leave
- workers who complain about these **sweatshop** conditions are denied **trade union rights** and sacked.

Shane doesn't want to be the odd one out.

Last term a friend was laughed at because of his cheap trainers.

Should Shane be pushed into buying a particular brand because of what his mates would say?

Or should he make a stand on this as a citizenship issue? Maybe he could explain his decision to his friends?

Living in a Global Economy
An example of how the system works:

1 Idea for trainers starts in a multinational company.
2 Money is borrowed from an American bank.
3 Trainers designed (e.g. in Germany).
4 Factories built and people employed (e.g. in Pakistan and Thailand).
5 Hong Kong company ships trainers.
6 Italian company designs the publicity/advertisements.
7 Finances/accounts/orders based in India.
8 Marketed in EU countries and the USA.
9 Distributed in Britain from headquarters in Birmingham.
10 Trainers sold in a chain of shops throughout the UK.

? Questions

1 Which factors would influence you when making citizenship decisions?
2 Explain what you would do if you were in Shane's position. Give reasons.

GLOSSARY

Eco-friendly: Products that do little or no damage to the environment.

Sweatshop: A factory where workers suffer long hours, low wages and poor conditions.

Trade union rights: The right to join with other workers to campaign for better pay/conditions.

Introduction

Rights and Responsibilities

KEY ISSUES

○ What are the rights and responsibilities of students, parents and teachers?

Do you have to go to school?
Can you choose your school?
What legal rights do you have?
What legal rights do your parents have?
What rights do schools have over students?
Read on to find out ....

Sandy says:

🗣 *I hate school*
🗣 *The work's too hard*
🗣 *I've no friends there*
🗣 *I get picked on*

Sandy often:

- says she is ill
- sets off for school but goes to the park or shops instead
- shouts at her mum and won't go
- gets found by the police and taken into school.

Her school has tried to:

- give her advice
- get her into school

- arrange support from the **Education Welfare Officer**.

But Sandy still won't go. Now Sandy's mum has got a letter. She will be taken to court. She is scared. Will she be fined? Could she be sent to prison?

What legal rights (backed by law) does the school have?

What legal responsibilities (backed by law) does Sandy's mum have as a parent to make her attend?

ⓘ INFO BOX

The Law says – Parents **must** make sure their children are educated full-time from 5–16. This can either be at school or 'otherwise' (e.g. taught at home). They must attend regularly. Parents can be prosecuted (taken to court), fined and as a last resort sent to prison if their child doesn't attend. It is no excuse to say they didn't know they were playing truant. It is no excuse to say they couldn't get them to attend. The police can take truants back to school. Schools should try to prevent bullying.

▲ Special officers look for children who should be at school.

Darrell is in Year 6. There is a good secondary school near his house. Nearly all his friends will go there. But Darrell likes the one 6.5 km away. It has an orchestra. It has great new computers.

 Role play the conversation between Darren and his parents about what to do for the best.

 INFO BOX

CAN YOU CHOOSE YOUR SCHOOL?

The Law says parents have the right to choose the school. But if it is full the school can refuse a place. If it is a Church school it may say no.

Home-School Agreement

The Rights and Responsibilities of parents, schools and students are set out in a Home–School Agreement such as this:

Staff and governors will try to:

- Teach students well
- Encourage them to achieve and behave
- Tell parents how their child is doing
- Welcome parents getting involved.

Parents will try to:

- Make sure their child attends on time and always has their books and equipment for the day
- Tell the school if there is a problem
- Support what the school says about behaviour and homework (its policy)
- Attend parents' evenings.

Students will try to:

- Arrive on time and always bring their books and equipment for the day
- Obey the school rules
- Wear correct uniform/keep the dress code
- Be polite and helpful.

PROJECT WORK

Compare your school's Home-School agreement with the one above.

Has your school kept to its side?

Have your parents kept to their side?

Have you kept to yours?

Which of the points do you think are most useful?

Which of the points do you think are least useful?

Does your School Council get a chance to discuss it?

▲ How should teachers show they are 'in loco parentis' (acting as a parent) on a field trip like this?

GLOSSARY

Education Welfare Officer: A person employed to help improve school attendance and punctuality.

? Questions

Give advice to Sandy and her mum. What do you think
a) Sandy should do?
b) Her mum should do?
c) Her school should do?
What do you think should happen if students don't attend school?

School Rules

Look at the picture of a Victorian schoolroom. Their rules were very strict. They said children must:

- stand when a teacher comes in
- call teachers Sir or Ma'am
- not ask questions
- sit and stand up straight
- be silent unless given permission to speak
- write using their right hand
- not use their fingers to count
- be on time and attend school regularly.

Do you think any of these rules were fair? Say why.

If the children broke any of these rules teachers had the right to cane them.

Some people say students get away with poor behaviour these days because schools don't have the right to use the cane. What do you think about this?

What kinds of punishment do you think are fair and effective?

▲ A typical Victorian classroom.

School Uniform Rules – True or False?

- Most schools have uniforms.
- It is the school governors who decide the uniform *policy*.
- Schools can insist you wear their uniform as long as it is reasonable.
- They can send you home if you don't wear it.
- They can fine your parents for non-attendance if you are not in school because you won't wear it.
- Schools can confiscate your jewellery.
- You can get it back eventually.
- Schools can make rules about haircuts, colours and styles.
- School uniform causes more disagreement and controversy than almost any other school rule.

All these statements are true

Uniform Protest

Year 10s at _____ School protested last week because they were **not** allowed to wear short trousers! They claimed it was so hot they should be allowed to have shorts. Things got ugly when some picked up rounders bats and refused to move back to lessons after break. A fire alarm was set off and the police were called.

Later the Head permanently excluded (expelled) two boys and one girl. Another ten have been given fixed term (temporary) exclusions.

The Head explained, 'Governors might have accepted the idea of shorts if it had come about in the proper way through school council and consultation. Some students took this too far and have been punished.'

In a separate incident Julie _____ was sent home for coming to school with a tongue stud. She complained, 'I got it fitted on holiday. They've told me not to come in until I've removed it.'

▲ Can students be suspended because of the style of their hair cut or colouring?

LOCKED OUT

Lisa knew that the rule was no eating or drinking in formrooms. But she was hungry and the dining room was full so she sneaked back to her formroom and ate her crisps. None of her other form mates noticed what she was doing.

'That's it Lisa. From now on I'm locking this door and no-one is allowed in over lunch. Out you all go,' said her form teacher.

'But why us,' the others moaned. 'We weren't doing anything .'

'Haven't you heard of **collective responsibility**?' came the reply.

▲ Students protesting about their money problems.

University education costs taxpayers a lot of money. To make students pay more of the costs, tuition fees have been introduced in England, Wales and Northern Ireland. From 2006 some universities will charge top-up fees of up to £3000 a year as well. This is on top of their living costs. Students will have to pay back the money when they get jobs. Some may have up to £25,000 of debt to pay off. The Government says this will be worth it because their degrees will get them higher paid jobs. Poorer students will get help towards their living expenses and fees.

Student Protest

Most students already complain about how hard up they are. As part of their organised campaign they have:

- slept out in a 'cardboard city' to make people aware of housing costs
- worn black armbands
- written their debts on balloons
- contacted their MPs and the media to express their opinions.

GLOSSARY

Collective responsibility: The whole group is responsible. If one member does something the others share the responsibility.

? Questions

1 Do you think it is fair that students are made to wear school uniform?
2 Was it fair that all the class were locked out of a classroom because of one individual's action?

KEY ISSUES

○ Who has power in school?
○ How can students influence decisions?

Who Runs the School?

Think of all the people who work in your school. It costs hundreds of thousands of pounds to staff and run a typical secondary school. Who runs the school? In State Schools it is:

1 Governors

The Governing body includes:

- Elected parent governors
- Local Education Authority (LEA) governors (often councillors or members of local political parties)
- Teacher governors elected by teaching staff
- A Staff governor elected by other school staff
- Co-opted governors (people who are invited to join because of their skills or links with the local community)
- The Headteacher.

Most Governors are part-time volunteers who take an interest in the school.

The role of the Governors is to:

- employ and recruit new staff
- decide on broad school policy
- oversee the school finances
- deal with complaints and hear appeals e.g. over exclusions.

2 School Staff

Each school may be run differently. Most secondary schools have:

- A Senior Management Team: Headteacher, Deputies, Assistant Heads. They make the main day-to-day executive decisions (like company directors or government ministers). The Head has the final responsibility for the leadership and direction of the school. The Head is accountable to the governing body and the Local Education Authority (LEA) for doing a good job. **OFSTED** inspectors also write public reports on the school and the quality of its leaders.

- Middle Management: Heads of Department/Faculty, Year Heads and Supervisors, e.g. Bursar, Catering Supervisor, Chief Caretaker. These staff are in charge of others and often have the power to make decisions over their area.

- Other Staff: Teachers, technicians, office staff, cleaning staff etc. Teachers manage their own classrooms.

Not all school staff have equal power or responsibility. But in practice Heads usually try to achieve a consensus (agreement) about the best thing to do. This means teaching staff can influence decisions through staff meetings and working parties.

3 Students

All school students are **stakeholders**. They are affected by what happens and so have an interest in how well the school is doing. About 50% of schools involve their students in decision-making through School Councils. How do these work?

▲ A school council meeting.

- Forms elect representatives.
- School council reps discuss issues democratically (trying to hear everyone's view). Some schools have class councils so that every form member can have a say before the School Council.
- The reps meet with the Senior Management to debate and put across their views. There is a two-way discussion.
- Decisions on items such as uniform, lunches, and improvement of facilities are often made in this way. But students don't always get what they want overnight.

4 Parents

Parents are also stakeholders. They can express their concerns at governors meetings and they can act as a pressure group for change if they think it is necessary. They can complain to the school, the Governors or the LEA if they disagree with a decision about their child.

GLOSSARY

OFSTED: Inspectors who make a public report back to parents, the LEA and the government about standards in each school.

Stakeholders: Those who are affected by what happens and so have an interest in how well the school is doing.

? Questions

1 Draw a diagram showing who has power in your school.
2 What role do governors have in your school? Find out some more about the sorts of decisions they make. You could arrange to talk to one of your school governors.
3 How far do students discuss things in your school? Say why you think school councils are/are not a good thing.

KEY ISSUES

○ How are schools involved in their local communities?
○ How does getting involved benefit students and others?

Schools are important in their local **communities**. Students can get more involved in local issues through school action. How?

1 Community Colleges

These secondary schools are open to adults as well as school students. Adults of all ages use the facilities in the evening and the daytime. Some courses are practical, such as gardening. Some courses give people a chance to get more qualifications or get better jobs. School students benefit by having bigger and better facilities than they would in an ordinary school. The community can use the facilities all the time. They aren't closed in the evenings.

▲ Students and adults at an evening class.

2 Community Schemes

Schools can be actively involved in projects involving their local communities and international issues.

Example: Waverley Council involved 39 local schools in planting native British trees like oaks. Students learned more about the environment and global warming. They also learned about groups like the World Wildlife Fund.

3 Working Together

School students can take the lead in local issues which benefit the whole community.

Example:

A class representative raised the issue of swimming – many students had never learned to swim because it was a rural area and there was no local pool.

↓

The School Council agreed it was a real problem and decided to approach others in the community.

↓

An Action Group was formed including councillors, parents, youth organisations, primary schools and businesses as well as school staff and students.

↓

The Group raised money from **grants** and **sponsorship**.

↓

The community built a new pool at the school.

↓

Everyone now uses the pool.

4 Local and International

School charity work can lead to international links and campaigns. Here's how it worked at one Devon school when a charity called 'Send a Cow' started to raise awareness.

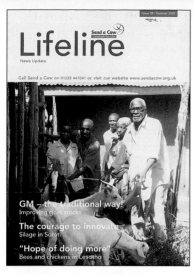

▲ The 'Send a Cow' newsletter keeps supporters informed.

▲ The school drum group performs in Uganda.

- A local charity worker thought 'Ugandan farmers need more cows ..... I'll ask the school students and local churches to help raise money.'

- The school students and staff said 'Goats, pigs and bees would be useful too.'

- The students and staff and parents thought 'Let's find out more about Uganda..... What can we learn from a Ugandan teacher visiting us?...... Maybe he could show us how to play African Drums?'

- The drum group suggested 'Let's visit Uganda ourselves.'

- The drum group said 'We'll link with schools out there.'

- The local doctor and nurses got involved too. 'We'll find out about their health needs.'

- The whole community decided 'We'll take clothing, toys and sports equipment too.'

- Everyone wanted to see for themselves what their involvement had led to.

- Everyone thought 'We'll get a lot out of it ourselves.'

GLOSSARY

Community: An area and the people who live there. People feel they belong there.

Grant: A gift of money from an organisation.

Sponsorship: A gift of money in return for benefits to the business such as favourable advertising.

? Questions

1 Do you think Community Colleges are a good idea? Explain your opinion.
2 What sorts of citizenship skills can school students learn from doing Community Schemes?
3 How can school action benefit a local community?
4 How can school students benefit from getting involved in charity work on global issues?
5 Investigate the links your school has with your local community.

Equality and Diversity

KEY ISSUES

○ What does the law say about equal opportunities?
○ How can schools promote equal opportunities for all?

There are several laws which protect individuals against **discrimination** (unfairly treating someone differently). The Human Rights Act 1998 banned all discrimination unless there is an extremely good reason for treating someone differently in a special case.

Schools also need to develop policies which promote the opportunities of all their students. These are called **Equal Opportunities policies**.

The Sex Discrimination Act

The Sex Discrimination Act 1975 said girls and boys should be treated equally.

So it is against the law for only girls to do cookery or only boys to do woodwork in DT lessons.

But schools think it is their job to go further. They want to make sure both girls and boys have the chance to develop all their skills and potential. They don't want boys to be **gender stereotyped** into science subjects or traditional 'men's' jobs. They don't want girls to be stereotyped into arts subjects or traditional 'women's' jobs (which are usually badly paid). And they want boys to achieve as well as girls at GCSE (In recent years 15% fewer boys than girls have achieved 5 GCSEs at Grade C or above).

Promoting equal opportunities for boys and girls

Which of these do you think is a good idea? Will it work? Say why.

- Encouraging girls to take up physics and engineering through **mentoring**, careers guidance and links with women scientists.

- Discouraging a laddish culture – where boys think it's not cool to work hard or behave responsibly – or pass their exams.

- Making sure lessons are more practical (boys are said to learn better this way).

- Cracking down on boys' disruptive behaviour (boys get more detentions and get excluded more often).

- Encouraging boys by providing good role models of men who have worked hard to achieve success.

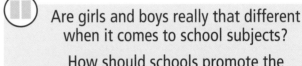

Are girls and boys really that different when it comes to school subjects?

How should schools promote the opportunities of girls **and** boys to make a success of their lives?

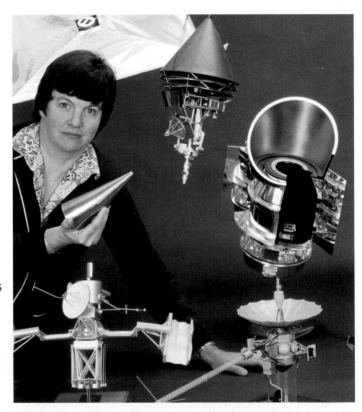

▲ A female engineer showing NASA spacecraft models.

Disability

Since 2002 it has been against the law to discriminate against people with a disability.

School governors have to say how their schools plan to meet the needs of disabled students.

Special Needs

Students with learning and behaviour difficulties are supported in school by SENCOS (Special Needs Coordinators) and teaching assistants. These students have a right to be fully included in the life of the school.

Religion and Schools

Religious discrimination is not covered by an Act of Parliament.

But state schools must provide religious education (RE). A school's RE syllabus is decided locally by representatives from different faith communities. This makes sure children grow up understanding the different religions. Parents can withdraw their children from RE. The majority religion in Britain is Christian. Some Christian faith groups run their own *voluntary aided schools* (religious state schools).

Faith groups would like more to be set up with their own identity e.g. Muslim, Jewish and Christian schools. Others say this would not help religious understanding. What do you think?

GLOSSARY

Discrimination: Treating people differently/not as well because of the group they belong to.

Equal Opportunities policies: Things schools do to try to give all their students a fair chance.

Gender stereotyping: Assuming all boys behave in a certain way and all girls behave in a different way.

Mentoring: Advising and supporting individual students.

? Questions

1 What do schools have to do for those students with special needs or disabilities?
2 Discuss whether girls and boys face gender stereotyping at school.
3 Do you think religious schools are a good idea? Explain your answer.

▲ A Muslim school in London.

Equality and Diversity

KEY ISSUES

○ What is a multicultural society?
○ How can we fight racial prejudice?

Our Multicultural Society

Britain is a multicultural country. This means it has different racial and cultural groups. Some have been here many centuries. Some are recent arrivals. Schools need to prepare students to understand the different cultures so we can respect differences.

❚❚ 11.3% of school students are from minority ethnic groups. What is the percentage in your school? Is this above or below the average nationally?

Perhaps your school has different minority cultures represented – e.g. people of Irish or Jewish or Cypriot descent?

In some schools most students are from ethnic minorities. In other schools no students are from ethnic minorities. This is because some areas are very multicultural (e.g. parts of London). Other areas are not (e.g. parts of Cornwall).

Why have people come to Britain? They may have come:

- to study
- to work (e.g. in the Health Service)
- to improve their chances in life
- to 'seek asylum' (because their government persecutes – seriously harrasses, imprisons, or hurts them)
- to join their family
- as visitors from the European Union or Commonwealth.

There are strict rules about immigration and who is allowed to stay here permanently.

But all schools want to encourage a community feeling and respect for others.

▲ Martin Luther King – American Civil Rights leader.

All schools want to discourage prejudice.

'I have a dream that my four little children will one day live in a nation where they will not be judged according to the colour of their skin but by the content of their character.'

Martin Luther King meant that racial prejudice (deciding someone is bad because of their skin colour) leads people to judge others wrongly

❚❚ Do you agree with his dream? How would you want to bring up your own children so they can live in a multicultural society?

ⓘ INFO BOX

THE LAW

The Race Relations Act of 1976 makes it against the law to

- **discriminate** (treat them differently/not as well) against anyone because of their race or colour
- harass, verbally abuse or assault people
- provoke racial hatred by what you say about them or write about them

Schools and school students are covered by these laws.

and to misunderstand what they are really like. His dream was to get rid of this prejudice.

Tina's Mistake

Tina was hot, thirsty and in a rush. At break she managed to buy a drink and some chocolate biscuits. She was really stressed. She grabbed the last seat in the canteen. But it was next to a male Indian student. She felt uneasy.

She opened the biscuits and took one. Then he smiled and took one! She felt cross but said nothing because there had been some trouble in school over race. She took another. So did he. Then he took the last biscuit, broke it in two and, with a big smile, gave her half.

Cheek! she thought, but she took it and went to her lesson. She complained about him to her friends using racist comments.

Then she found her chocolate biscuits in her bag. She had eaten his biscuits! She felt ashamed.

▲ 'He helped himself to my chocolate biscuits!'

Why had Tina assumed the worst about him?

Was she racially prejudiced?

What could she do to make things right?

How can we tackle our own prejudices?

How can we cope with people who are from different cultures to our own?

? Questions

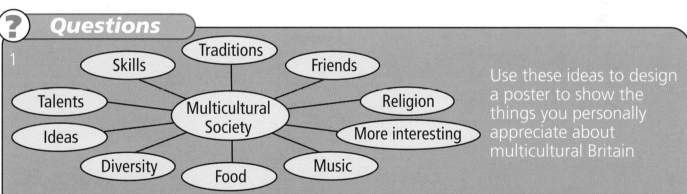

1 Skills, Traditions, Friends, Talents, Religion, Multicultural Society, More interesting, Ideas, Diversity, Music, Food

Use these ideas to design a poster to show the things you personally appreciate about multicultural Britain

2 Are people from different cultures made to feel welcome? Find out about attitudes to immigrants. You could ask people whether they agree or disagree with the following views:
'Britain needs more immigrants. We are short of skilled people.'
'There are too many illegal immigrants. People smugglers are making a fortune.'
'Newcomers face prejudice in this area.'
'Immigrants work hard and do their new country a lot of good.'
'Once here the law must protect all its citizens from racism.'

3. Research the experiences of people from different ethnic minorities who have come here on www.movinghere.org.uk.

Rights and Responsibilities

KEY ISSUES

- ○ What rights and responsibilities do employers and employees have?
- ○ What laws are there to help people achieve equal opportunities at work?

Meet Sadie. She:

- works in a grocery shop
- is employed by Mr Duckworth
- has been employed part-time for 2 years
- is the only black worker in a staff of 12.

Sadie is happy at work. But Mr Duckworth tells her she must work every Sunday morning. She refuses because she goes to church on Sundays. He sacks her.

Can she claim unfair dismissal?

Is there anything else she can do to protect her rights at work?

Look at the following table of general laws to find out.

Might help Sadie	Definitely will help Sadie	All employees can
✓		a) join a trade union and ask it for help
		b) have time off for **jury service**
		c) claim equal pay for similar work between men and women (Equal Pay Act)
✓		d) expect employers not to treat them unfairly because of their race (Race Relations Act 1995), disability (Disability Discrimination Act 1995) or sex (Sex Discrimination Act 1975)
		e) claim 18 weeks maternity pay
	✓	f) have the right not to be dismissed for refusing to work on Sunday (Sunday Trading Act 1994)
		After a month at work employees can
✓		g) be paid if laid off
✓		h) have 1 week's notice of dismissal
		After two months at work employees can
✓		i) have a written statement of employment
		After a year at work employees can
✓		j) claim unfair dismissal
		k) claim **redundancy pay** if the job isn't needed any more
✓		l) have the same rights as full-time workers if they are part-time

Trade Unions

Trade Unions might help in all three of the cases described in this section. Unions negotiate with employers, help sort out disputes, give legal advice and campaign for better pay and conditions. They charge their members *dues* – money that pays for services such as legal advice and strike pay.

Meet Narinder. She:

- has worked 20 years in the same company
- is well qualified
- was promoted at first.

But now Narinder is near the top of the company she has not got the promotions she has applied for. Men with less good qualifications and experience have been given them. She suspects this is because she is a woman and has hit a '**glass ceiling**'.

Look again at the table on Page 18. What rules/laws might help Narinder?

Answer:

a), c) and d) might help. She could bring a case under the Equal Pay Act or the Sex Discrimination Act or the Race Relations Act. A trade union would give her advice and support her. But it is hard to prove this sort of discrimination.

National Minimum Wage

Employers must not pay less than the National minimum wage. It applies to **all** employees over 21 wherever they work. The rate in 2003 was £4.25 an hour. This benefits nearly 2 million low paid workers.

Meet Craig. He:

- is 22
- is a Factory Worker
- earns £3.90 an hour
- does unpaid overtime as well.

His boss says he can't afford to pay him any more or jobs will be lost.

> **||** Is Craig covered by the law on the National Minimum Wage? What other laws might help him?

GLOSSARY

Glass ceiling: Describes what happens to some women and black workers who don't get promotion to the top jobs because of unseen attitudes and discrimination.

Jury service: Anyone over 18 on the electoral register can be called to serve as a juror, listen to the evidence and decide whether someone is guilty or not guilty.

Redundancy payment: A lump sum payment when someone loses their job because the company cuts jobs, moves the place of work or closes down.

? Questions

1. Explain how Craig's employer is breaking the law.
2. Do you think the law gives enough protection against unfair dismissal? Give reasons for your answer.
3. Do you think there are equal opportunities for men and women in employment? How helpful are the laws on this?

KEY ISSUES

○ What must employers do to promote health and safety?
○ What protection do workers have?

 Which areas of a school are likely to be covered in a COSHH survey?

The Control of Asbestos at Work Regulations now cover asbestos illnesses. This is because in the past asbestos caused such long term damage that over 1800 people died from it in 1999 alone. These workers can claim compensation if it was the company's fault.

When there is an accident which causes the worker to be off work for more than 3 days employers must tell the Health and Safety Executive or local authority.

In 2000–2001 106 out of the 295 deaths were in the construction industry. 73 people died falling from heights. 46 deaths were in the agriculture industry.

Deaths were caused by moving vehicles, falling objects and things collapsing or overturning.

NEWS REPORT

Court fines company £628,000 for death of two workers

Leicester Crown Court has found Harvestine Bakery guilty of breaking the Health and Safety at Work Act 1974. They had not used specialists to repair their giant oven. Instead they sent in two of their own workers while it was still too hot. The men died and the directors were found to be responsible.

Health and Safety at Work Act

This law means all employers must 'as far as reasonably possible' make sure the working environment is safe.

This covers removing hazards, e.g.

- Putting up guards round dangerous machinery
- Stopping machinery before it is cleaned
- Making sure the air is safe to breathe
- Providing safe ladders/cranes
- Cleaning workplaces so people don't trip or slip
- Providing clothing and helmets to protect workers
- Reducing the noise level or protecting workers' ears
- Training workers to lift safely

Employers (including schools) must carry out **risk assessments** to identify hazards.

Employers must also fill in a COSHH survey. This identifies any 'control of substances hazardous to health' such as poisons, acids, and corrosive liquids.

◀ Health and safety issues are very important in many occupations.

Employees

As an employee you must 'take reasonable care' of your own health and safety and that of others while at work. If you are careless or mess about and cause an accident you are responsible. You could be prosecuted if your *negligence* hurt someone else.

Work Experience Safety Issues

You will have to deal with health and safety issues when you do work experience.

Julie is looking forward to her first day at a local garage. She wants to get a **modern apprenticeship** in engineering when she leaves school. She knows a good reference would help her.

But she finds there are many hazards. There are things blocking the corridors and metal objects she could trip over. She has never used some of the equipment like welding gear. Someone asks her to move some heavy metal and try some welding.

She thinks:

- *Will I do my back in?*
- *Do I know enough about this welding gear?*
- *Where are the goggles?*
- *Should I wear gloves?*
- *Where's the fire extinguisher?*

GLOSSARY

Modern apprenticeship: A paid training placement in a company where you learn on the job.

Risk assessment: Possible hazards (things that could go wrong or be dangerous) are described. The hazards are removed or staff are given ways of dealing with them.

? Questions

1 Which of the following would be good ideas for someone in Julie's shoes? Explain your answers.

- Down tools and go home

- Ring your mum

- Watch what the others do and copy them

- Start the job even though you're not sure

- Storm off to complain

- Find your supervisor and explain exactly why you are worried about health and safety

- Ask for training and practice

- Point out the hazards you have noticed and ask what the advice is in the risk assessment for coping with them

- Politely but firmly insist that you will not start any task you think could hurt yourself or others

- If still worried, ring school to ask advice

Work in Motion

KEY ISSUES
❍ How does work affect the economy?
❍ How do financial services work?

Anne Marie's work experience placement was in a local factory that makes microchips for computers.

When she got back to school she made a spider diagram. This shows the way companies affect the whole economy. We are all affected by our local and national economy.

1 Microchips and the new technologies

Microchips are now cheap and tiny. Nearly all companies in Britain use microchips and computers in many ways. This has led to new companies such as mobile phone and internet businesses growing up over the last ten years. Businesses have changed over to electronic methods because computing is now fast, efficient and convenient.

5 Financial services

a) Business finance
Companies are owned by shareholders. These shares can be bought or sold on the Stock Exchange. Shareholders earn **dividends** from the profits.

Every year there is an **audit** of the accounts to present to shareholders. Companies can be taken over (bought) by others – either British or foreign firms.

Companies can borrow money from banks. They must pay back interest as well as the capital (original amount).

Companies and banks make payments by electronic transfer. They convert currency to buy and sell from abroad.

b) Personal finance
Individuals can save money in banks and building societies. Withdrawals are usually made by debit card, direct debit or cheque. You can buy and sell shares and have pension funds or other ways of investing in the stock market.

Money can be borrowed from a bank or building society in the following ways:

• mortgage (to buy a house)
• overdraft/personal loan (for a short term loan)
• credit card e.g. VISA (to make purchases or withdraw cash here and abroad).

You have to pay interest on loans. The rate varies according to your credit rating (how much of a risk you are) and what the Base Rate of the Bank of England is.

4 Taxes

Two taxes are deducted (taken straight from wage packets) by employers. These are **direct taxes** – they go straight to the government. All employees pay them. They are Income Tax and National Insurance. The more you earn, the more you pay. The Government spends the money on services for the country such as the National Health Service, the armed forces and the state retirement pension.

You pay other **indirect taxes** as well to the national government. Everyone who buys the goods (not just working people) pays VAT (Value Added Tax) and other taxes such as those on petrol, alcohol, cigarettes and Vehicle tax. The Government can change these taxes in its Budget when it increases or reduces its spending for the year.

Council tax is paid to your local council based on the value of property. This helps pay for education, the police and other services provided by local authorities.

2 A modern company

Companies like Anne Marie's employ hundreds of workers. The company is organised into different sections to do what is necessary e.g.

- manufacturing (making the microchip)
- supplying local firms which assemble computers
- selling the chips to other British firms and exporting chips abroad
- dealing with customers
- finance (making sure customers pay and outgoings are covered)
- transport
- stock control
- wages

3 The local community

The company plays an important part in the local economy e.g.

- employing local people and paying their wages
- buying goods and services from other local businesses, which also employ people
- making the area richer when employees spend their wages locally

If the company closed it would have a bad 'knock on effect' – other firms would suffer from the loss of jobs and wages.

If the company expanded it would have a good 'knock on effect' – other firms do well too when more money comes in to the local economy.

GLOSSARY

Audit: When company accounts are examined to see if they are correct.

Direct taxes: Money taken straight from wages to pay for the national government.

Dividend: Money paid to shareholders who have invested in a company.

Indirect taxes: Money for the national government that you pay when you buy things.

? Questions

1 Could it be dangerous for a town to rely on just one main industry? Explain why. Give an example of a local area that has suffered in this way.
2 Make a list of the big companies and employers in your area. What do they make or provide?
3 Look at the financial pages of a national newspaper or BBCi homepage (www.bbc.co.uk: Click BBC News. Click Business) Use it to answer the following questions.
   a) What is the exchange rate of the pound against the Euro?
   b) Has the FTSE 100 (share price of top 100 British companies) gone up or down?
4 Look at a till receipt. How much VAT was paid?

The Business World

A strong economy is important because it creates jobs and increases demand for jobs and services.

A time when this happens is called an expansion or period of growth.

In a weak economy you see:

• companies closing
• jobs lost through redundancy
• less demand for goods and services.

A time when this happens is called a recession.

Some parts of the economy are usually stronger than other parts.

Example: In the nineteenth century British **primary** and **secondary industries** expanded fast. In the twenty-first century **tertiary industries** have taken over.

Less developed economies usually rely on **primary** or **secondary** industries. They can often compete well making factory goods because their wages are less. This is why many British manufacturing jobs have gone.

More developed economies need well educated people to work in their service industries (also called tertiary industries). New technologies can produce well paid jobs.

Coal mining is a primary industry. Nearly all Britain's deep coal mines have now shut. There are very few miners left. Traditional coal mining areas have been hit hard by unemployment and recession.

Steel-making is a secondary industry. Very little steel is now made in Britain. Traditional steel-making areas like South Wales have had to change over to other newer industries.

▲ Open cast mining – an example of a primary industry.

▲ A textile factory – an example of a secondary industry.

▲ Tourism – an example of a service or tertiary industry.

In Manchester the old textile industry has been overtaken by new service industries like banking, retail, tourism and education.

Computer Power

Computers and other new technologies have created economic growth and jobs.

Here's how it works

There are both manufacture and service jobs.

Manufacture: Microchips are made and sent to other countries where computers are assembled.

Service Industry: Different companies have sprung up to provide services in computer applications e.g. software design and web page design. Business companies export (sell their services to other countries).

The actual computer is **imported** into Britain. Britain pays for it.

The services are **exported** to other countries. They pay for them. As long as Britain exports as much as it imports there is no **balance of payments problem**.

Many new jobs involve computing. They include managing the database, desktop publishing, and word processing.

This helps the economy grow because these people earn money for:

- Themselves (wages)
- Their local areas (council tax, and buying things locally)
- Their country (national taxes and exports)

Other industries which have been boosted by computers include marketing on the internet and entertainment e.g. Playstations and games.

Several computer companies have their headquarters in Britain.

Criterion Software develops and sells the software to make games.

Criterion Games develops the games themselves – the characters, artwork, sound and music for Nintendo Gamecube and Sony Playstation 2.

They sell the original 'gold disks' to multinational publishers like Sony. Sony produces hundreds of thousands of them. A distributor sends them to retailers around the world. An advertising campaign markets them.

Criterion has to keep developing new ideas to keep ahead of the competition and stay in business.

PROJECT WORK

1 Look in the Situations Vacant section of your local newspaper. Are the jobs available mainly in primary, secondary or service industries?

2 How many of the jobs seem to use computers and new technologies?

3 Find out about new technologies in your area. Look under computers in your Yellow Pages (or online). Count the number of sections e.g. computer maintenance, computer aided design. Make sure you know what these mean.

GLOSSARY

Balance of payments problem: When a country imports more than it exports.

Export: Send goods abroad.

Import: Bring foreign goods into a country.

Primary industries: Farming, mining, quarrying, fishing. These industries directly produce raw materials or food.

Secondary industries: These industries manufacture goods from raw materials.

Tertiary industries: These industries provide services; they don't make things in factories.

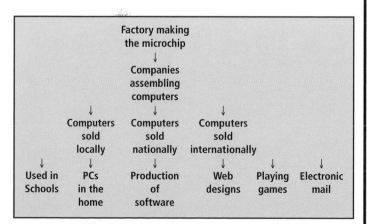

▲ The 'ripple effect' of computers.

Ethnic Groups

KEY ISSUES

○ How can race, religion or culture be a problem between communities?

Sometimes there are tensions between different ethnic groups. Why? Why do violence and riots happen?

Example: During 2001 there were serious racial attacks in Bradford. Asian and white people were stabbed. Then two hundred rioters, many of them young Asian men, took to the streets. Hundreds of (mainly white) police officers tried to control them. Police in riot gear were hit by bricks and petrol bombs. Over a hundred were injured. Thirty-six people were arrested, including thirteen Asians. The riots spread to other towns. There were over 150 arrests.

Afterwards people said:

- 🗣 *Racists in the National Front and the British National Party deliberately stirred up trouble between Asians and whites.*
- 🗣 *There aren't enough ethnic minority officers in the police.*
- 🗣 *These young men were poor and disadvantaged.*
- 🗣 *These young men were hotheads who wanted a fight.*
- 🗣 *These areas had housing problems. Council estates were nearly all white. Other areas were nearly all Asian. People didn't mix in schools or socially. Suspicion and conflicts grew.*
- 🗣 *The Council hadn't done enough to make services like good schools, youth clubs and jobs available fairly to all the community.*

⏸ Which of these is the best explanation?

What do you think would help improve community relations in places like Bradford?

▲ Riots due to racial tension in Bradford, 2001.

Arranged Marriages

In Britain most people get married for love. Individuals find their own partners. Parents don't expect to have much of a say. But in some ethnic groups, it is part of their culture to have arranged marriages. Parents choose the partners.

▲ In many cultures marriages are traditionally arranged.

What are the advantages and drawbacks of arranged marriges?

For:	Against:
– They help keep the traditions and religion going. – They help keep **extended families** going. – Couples may move in with the husband's parents so children and old people are looked after by the family. – Couples are less likely to divorce because they are from the same background. – Family support is there if things go wrong. – Young people are protected from the problems of teenage sex, unwanted pregnancy and unhappy break-ups.	– Young people brought up in this country watch TV and are influenced by their friends. They may want a love marriage. – Young people can argue with their parents over this. – Sometimes conflict leads to breaking the laws of this country and violence if a marriage is forced. – It can be hard for young people to accept why they can't just go out with someone from an ethnic minority which practices arranged marriage

Different Customs and Religions

It can be hard to be different from the majority. British laws and customs might not let you follow your religion or your traditions easily (e.g. festivals of other faiths don't fall within school holidays). Some people are prejudiced or feel threatened by minority customs. Do you think minorities should have to change in order to fit in? Should majorities accept and value differences between people? How can the human rights of ethnic minorities be protected?

Which of these opinions do you agree with? Say whether you Agree/Disagree or are Not Sure. Which would help improve community relations? Explain why.

- 🗣 *'All ethnic minorities in Britain should learn English.*
- 🗣 *Children should be banned from speaking any other language than English in the playground.*
- 🗣 *Muslims should have the right to attend mosque on Fridays and take time off for Festivals such as Eid-ul-Fitr when they fall on a working day.*
- 🗣 *Sunday should be a working day just like any other day. So should Christmas.*
- 🗣 *Schools and restaurants should serve halal, kosher or vegetarian food to anyone who asks for it.*
- 🗣 *People should be able to wear what they like if it is part of their religion.*

GLOSSARY

Extended family: Not just parents and children but grandparents, uncles, aunts etc

? Questions

1 List the difficulties that immigrants face when settling into a new country.
2 Aisha is a young person who wishes to maintain her culture and family traditions by accepting a marriage arranged by her parents. Charlie is a young person who thinks love marriages are much better. Role play their discussion.

Think of some of the culture and celebrations which different ethnic minorities have brought to Britain. This has made the country a much more interesting place to live. The variety has added colour and excitement to life here.

The Queen said this:

> *'Welcoming diversity is not just about tolerating (putting up with) difference.*
> *Living together as neighbours needs more than that.*
> *We must reach out, recognise and welcome difference.*
> *We should accept that we have duties as well as rights.*
> *We should seek to leave the world a better place.*
> *This requires respect for others and a readiness to learn from them.*
> *By doing this we enrich our own lives.'*

(adapted from Elizabeth R, 11 March 2002).

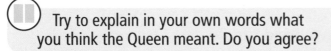

Try to explain in your own words what you think the Queen meant. Do you agree?

Chinese New Year

The date of the Chinese New Year varies from late January to the middle of February (it depends on the moon's cycle). This Spring festival celebrates the earth coming back to life.

Within the Chinese community they clean their homes, repay debts, cut their hair and buy new clothes. Good luck messages on red paper decorate the doors of their houses, colourful lanterns decorate the rooms and charms are hung up to keep away evil spirits. Families burn incense as a mark of respect to ancestors. On New Year's Eve a large family dinner is served and the houses are brightly lit. At midnight fireworks are lit to drive away

▲ Prince Charles celebrates a Muslim festival with young people from the British Islamic community.

evil spirits. New Year's day is spent visiting neighbours, family and friends.

In many big cities everyone can get involved in the street celebrations. Chinatown has stalls selling things like paper dragons, Chinese toys, and Chinese food. Firecrackers are lit and Chinese dragons are paraded in the streets with the beating of a drum and gongs.

▲ Chinese New Year.

The Notting Hill Carnival

The Notting Hill Carnival began in London when West Indian immigrants moved into the area. In Trinidad the carnival tradition is very strong. The black community (particularly immigrants from Trinidad) and local people wanted to create a festival to bring together the people of Notting Hill.

This three-day carnival takes place each August Bank Holiday weekend. Up to two million people celebrate the diverse cultures that make up multi-cultural Britain. It is the biggest carnival outside of Rio and it is very noisy and colourful.

40,000 masqueraders parade through the 'biggest street party in Europe'. People of different cultures and backgrounds party and mix together. They enjoy the colourful costumes and floats but the music makes it special. Music at the carnival comes from sound systems playing Soca and Reggae, steel bands and Calypso. People dress in **masquerade** or 'mas'. You can buy food and drink, including jerk chicken, sweet corn and pig's trotters, from the stalls that line the streets.

Some complain the Carnival is now too big for the area. Many others enjoy this huge multi-cultural arts festival.

▲ Notting Hill Carnival.

Practising Faith

Ethnic minorities find their religion helps keep their community alive even in a new country.

In the **gurdwara**:

- Sikhs worship and have their community centre

- young people learn to read and write Punjabi
- mother and toddler groups and lunch clubs for senior citizens are held
- after their service, worshippers gather for *langar*, the community meal prepared in their kitchen.

By worshipping and eating together the Sikh community shares each other's problems and give each other support. They are demonstrating their belief that all people are equal.

The closeness of ethnic groups has allowed traditions to survive for hundreds of years in foreign countries. A Jewish state did not exist for nearly two thousand years, but their religion and way of life was kept alive in the communities where Jews lived.

GLOSSARY

Gurdwara: A Sikh temple and social centre.

Masquerade: Costumes from a West Indian street parade.

? Questions

1 Name some of the main ethnic minority groups in Britain.
2 Think about different celebrations such as the Chinese New Year and the Notting Hill Carnival. Explain how they can help to bring tolerance and understanding between different ethnic communities.
3 Explain why members of ethnic minorities often live in close-knit communities. Mention tradition, families, language and support.
4 Britain has become a much more colourful and interesting society because of the influence of ethnic and religious minorities. Do you agree? Give reasons.

Ethnic Groups

Power and Authority

▲ Refuse collection is just one of the services the Council provides.

Why do we need local government?

What if there were no services like police or libraries? We need government to provide these. But the Government does not want to run everything from London. Local people don't want this either. Why is this? Rank the following reasons in order of importance.

- What matters in one area might not matter somewhere else.
- Local people who know about their area can get involved (**participate**).
- Local councils can identify the specific needs of the local community and its people.
- London and central government are more remote and difficult to contact. It is more convenient and efficient to run things locally.
- If things go wrong people want local officials on hand to put them right.
- If services are poor they need local **representatives** (councillors) to work to improve them.
- Elected Councillors are **accountable** for problems and can be voted out in local elections without waiting for General Elections which may be up to 5 years away.
- Local **democracy** means people can make choices about who runs their area.

What local government can do

The real power stays with the central government in Westminster. Parliament makes the laws which control what local government does.

There are some things it *must* do. They are *obligatory*. Examples:

- maintain the public highways (mend the roads).

- deal with planning applications (to put up new buildings such as house extensions).

There are some things it *may* do. They are *permissive*. Example: support the Arts in a local area.

PROJECT WORK

1 Imagine there were no local government and everything was run from London. How would you feel about this? What would you complain about most?

2 Look at any Council Tax Bill. List the main services provided by your council. Which department:

- provides home helps for the elderly and sick?
- keeps the environment clean and safe?
- collects the refuse and disposes of dangerous waste?
- runs schools?
- runs Leisure Centres?
- runs libraries?
- grits or salts the roads in winter?

The main government department that oversees local councils in England is the Department of Transport, Local Government and the Regions (DTLR). Well over half the money spent by local councils comes from central government and is paid for by national taxes.

▲ Ken Livingstone campaigning to become Mayor of London in 2000.

ℹ️ INFO BOX

WHO DOES WHAT?

In England there are three main types of local authority (council).

- Single-tier (unitary). One council runs all services.
- Two-tier. County councils run county-wide services like education. District councils run more local services like waste collection and parking.
- Metropolitan. There are 36 metropolitan areas. These cities have big councils which run all services.

ℹ️ INFO BOX

LONDON

The largest metropolitan authority is the Greater London Authority (GLA). The London boroughs like Camden run most services. But London also has the GLA to look after things which affect all Londoners including:

- economic development
- environment
- fire and emergency planning
- transport e.g. the GLA can charge motorists a 'congestion charge' for taking their car into the centre of London. This encourages the use of public transport.
- planning
- police (through the Police Authority).

Londoners elect their own mayor and assembly to run the GLA.

GLOSSARY

Accountable: Must explain their decisions to the public.

Democracy: The people choose.

Participate: Get actively involved.

Representative: Someone who is elected to make decisions.

❓ Questions

1. Do you live in a two-tier or a single-tier or a single-tier metropolitan authority? Explain the difference.
2. Would it be a good idea to have a directly elected mayor in your area? Explain why/why not.
3. Do you think people in your area know enough about your local council? Write down some questions to ask and conduct a survey amongst adults and young people.

Power and Authority

KEY ISSUES

- ❍ Who pays for local authorities?
- ❍ How do the councils work?
- ❍ Should there be regional assemblies for England?

Big Spenders

Local authorities (councils) spend about £70 billion every year – a quarter of all the money that is spent on public services. It's a lot of money! It comes from four main sources:

1 National taxes like income tax and VAT. Central government gives councils a slice of this each year called the revenue support grant.
2 Non-domestic rates – a tax on business premises.
3 Council Tax – a tax on peoples' homes based on the house's value.
4 Revenue (from charges) e.g. parking.

Councils employ over two million people. After several meetings, the full council usually meets in February for a special meeting to agree the budget for the next twelve months and to set the Council Tax.

Who Runs the Councils?

The councils are run by paid **officers** and elected **councillors**.

▲ A full council sets the Council Tax.

COUNCILLORS

Most councillors are only paid expenses. They have other jobs too.

The councillors decide on policy – they accept, change or reject what the officers have suggested.

The councillors are members of the community who are elected by voters in their *Ward*.

Most councillors stand for a political party but some are independent.

There are more than 20,000 local councillors. They make important decisions each day which affect the lives of people in the local community.

Councillors' duties include:

- making decisions at meetings;
- helping **constituents** with their problems – they hold 'surgeries' where residents arrange to see them;
- visiting or telephoning constituents and then speaking or writing to council officials to try and get problems sorted;
- attending other meetings such as school governor meetings to represent the council or their constituents and find out information to assist them in their job.

OFFICERS

Officers are appointed to carry out (execute) the major decisions made by the councillors. The top officer is called the chief executive.

Officers oversee the day to day running of the council. Officers prepare reports and agendas for the councillors and recommend ideas for the councillors to consider.

Officers are paid and full-time. They are non-political.

The Full Council

The whole council can decide things in a Full Committee. This meets in the council chamber and usually sits in a horseshoe shape facing the chairman of the council. Most councillors belong to a political group and they usually sit in their groups.

Decisions are first considered by committees or sub-committees e.g. the Education Committee. These also check how effective the services are and take action to improve things when there are problems.

The leader of the council is called the chairman or, in some cases, the mayor of a town or borough. The chairman is the leader of the largest party group on the council. Also they entertain important visitors and represent the council on formal occasions.

Regional Assemblies?

Scotland has its own parliament. Wales and London have assemblies. Should English regions such as the North West also run themselves? The Government has set up eight English regional development agencies to try to improve the regional economies. These are based in the north-east, north-west, west midlands, east midlands, south-east, south-west and the eastern regions. Will eight directly elected regional assemblies follow?

Regional Assemblies, Yes or No? Which of these opinions do you agree with?

✓ More people live in each English region than in Scotland or Wales. They should have devolution so they can run things their way.

✗ It is unnecessary; the English don't feel that strongly about their regions.

✓ It would bring money and jobs to the regions. Regions would be better at getting grants and aid from the London government and the European Union.

✗ It is too expensive; more offices and officers would be needed.

✓ It would help people participate democratically in their own regions.

✗ There would be too many tiers of government. County councils would need to be abolished. Single-tier authorities would need to be set up instead.

GLOSSARY

Constituents: People who live in the ward.

Devolution: Central government at Westminster transfers power to the regions, in order to give local people a bigger say in the decisions which affect their areas.

Wards: An area of the local authority. Councillors represent all the residents of the ward. They are elected by the voters of their ward and are accountable to them.

? Questions

1 Explain the differences between the role of a local government officer and a councillor.
2 Does devolution to the regions get your vote?

How Can Individuals Bring About Change?

KEY ISSUES

○ How does democracy work?
○ How does a person become a councillor?

Standing for Election

One way of bringing about change is to become an elected representative. As a councillor, you are able to influence the decisions that are taken by the local government.

'...democratic election gives local councillors a special status...It is no easy task being a local councillor...Certainly no councillor would seek election in order to get rich...but the ambition to serve on a council remains an honourable calling and should be recognised as such.' (Lord Nolan's Report on Standards of Conduct in Local Government)

Who wants to be a Councillor?

Councillors are elected for four years. Elections usually take place on the first Thursday of May. If a councillor resigns, or dies, a person is elected to fill the vacancy in a by-election.

In some authorities elections are held every year and a third of the seats are filled each time.

In other authorities all the councillors are elected at the same time every fourth year.

WANTED – PERSON WHO WOULD MAKE A GOOD COUNCILLOR

Must care about the area and want to help people Councillors serve the public interest.

Must be honest It would be dishonest to use the position to gain financial benefits for themselves or their friends. Decisions should be made on merit, not because a family friend has tendered for a council contract. To accept a bribe or award a contract as a favour would be corruption.

Must abide by the law Councillors have a duty to uphold the law.

Must make wise decisions They should help the council make the right decisions and not waste money.

Must know their own minds Leadership qualities, and the ability to persuade and communicate opinions are important, as councillors often have to lead campaigns to get things changed.

Must listen to public opinion Councillors who fail to listen to their electors or do not work hard for their areas are likely to lose their seats to another candidate when the elections are held.

ⓘ INFO BOX

You can become a Councillor if you:

- are 21 or over on the day of nomination
- do not have criminal convictions
- have property in or work connections within the Council area
- are a UK, Commonwealth or EU citizen
- have not been declared bankrupt
- do not work for the council for whom you wish to be a councillor.

Most candidates stand for election with the backing of a political party e.g. Conservative, Green, Labour or Liberal Democrat. Those who do not are known as Independents.

Seeking Election – Here are the stages you have to go through as a candidate

1 Be nominated by electors in the ward you are standing for.

2 Hand in the Nomination papers by the required date.

3 Campaign. This involves you and your helpers producing leaflets, which are delivered to the electors. These leaflets give personal details about your experience and involvement in

▲ A candidate canvassing for support.

community life and why you seek election. Electors need to know your policies on the key campaign issues.

4 Canvass for support by calling on voters. Try and persuade the electors to turn out and vote for you on polling day.

Choosing a Councillor – Here are the stages you have to go through as a voter

1 **Get yourself on the Electoral Register**. When you are 18 fill in the form sent by your Council. They will send you a polling card a few weeks before the election telling you where your polling station is/how to make a postal vote.

2 **Go to your polling station** on election day.

3 **Take a ballot paper**. Go to the poll booth (an area set up so people can vote in secret).

4 **Put a cross against the candidate you want**. (Do not write anything else or your vote will be 'spoilt' and not count).

5 **Put your ballot paper in the ballot box**. At the end of the election the ballot boxes are sealed and taken to the count for checking. After the papers are counted the returning officer announces the result. In England the 'first past the post system' is used, which means that the candidate with the highest number of votes is declared the winner.

GLOSSARY

Electoral register: A list of those who are entitled to vote.

Postal vote: The elector is issued with a ballot paper before the election and posts their vote to the returning officer.

Tender: A costed bid to run a council service.

▲ Primary schools are sometimes used as polling stations.

? Questions

1 Explain in your own words what Lord Nolan meant.

2 Make a list of the qualities needed to be a councillor. Put them in order of what you think are the most important. Explain why you have chosen this order

3 Why might a person want to be a local councillor? Think about getting involved, making a difference locally, and political beliefs.

How Can Individuals Bring About Change?

How Can You as an Individual Bring About Change?

1 Know and use your rights as a citizen

You live in a council house which needs repairing. There are problems with the bath and toilet. What could you do?

Council tenants have rights as laid down in the tenant's charter. Urgent repairs should be done quickly at no charge.

- Step One: contact the local housing office and explain the problem is urgent. Hopefully the problem will then be solved. If this doesn't work, use the council's complaints procedure.
- Step Two: if this hasn't worked, ask for help and advice from your local councillor.
- Step Three: if the council hasn't done its job properly you could contact the local government ombudsman (an independent investigator).
- Step Four: if the problem is still not sorted out you could seek legal advice.

If the behaviour of your neighbours is a problem you can complain to the council. It is easier for the council to take action if your neighbours are council tenants (because it could evict them if they are found guilty of using the council house for 'immoral or illegal purposes'). Otherwise the Environmental Health Department will try to sort out problems like noise or rubbish. The police and council can prosecute for anti-social behaviour if they have enough evidence. Getting together with other neighbours is very useful.

2 Persuade those with power to change the system

Case Study – How to get active in Green issues

- find out more about the issue you care about (read, listen to people).
- Use your influence with friends or workmates to gain their support and spread the message.
- Campaign for change by contacting those who have power – could be local or national politicians, businesses, or public bodies like the National Rivers Authority.
- Use your vote to support politicians/ political parties who agree with you.
- Take part in/organise protests against pollution, deforestation, etc.
- Use your consumer power e.g. refuse unnecessary packaging, cycle/walk/avoid using a car, boycott companies which pollute and exploit, eat organic foods.
- Recycle your waste paper, glass, metals; don't leave litter.
- Write to M.P.'s or the press.
- Join pressure groups e.g. Friends of the Earth or Greenpeace.

Be aware that your campaign for a particular cause may not be successful. People may not agree with you. Perhaps it isn't an issue for them or they may not care.

3 Join a Pressure Group

It can help to join with other people who think like you do. Groups that campaign to change things that affect us as citizens are called pressure groups.

1. Some groups are set up by individuals who realise things need changing when they are personally affected.
2. Some groups are set up to campaign on a single issue. For example, the Dunblane campaign was successful in getting Parliament to tighten up gun control (see page 76).
3. Local groups can form when needed e.g. to stop the council closing an old peoples' home.
4. Some groups have become national or even international pressure groups:
   - Campaign for Nuclear Disarmament (CND)

▲ Esther Rantzen became President of the Association of Young People with ME after her daughter began suffering from the disease.

- National Abortion Campaign
- The Society for the Protection of the Unborn Child (SPUC)
- Amnesty International. Started by a small group of volunteers in a little office in London, Amnesty International has now become the world's largest international voluntary organisation campaigning for human rights.

Shelter

▲ Shelter is a pressure group that campaigns about the problems of the homeless.

4 Join a Voluntary Organisation

Like-minded people often get together to form their own voluntary groups. The work they do is usually unpaid. People give up their time to make these groups work. 21 million people in the UK take part in at least one voluntary activity, giving more than 85 million hours per week to it. They meet other people and enjoy making a contribution. England has about 200,000 different voluntary organisations:

1 Many of these are local or national charities that raise money for good causes. In 1999 their income was over £13 billion.

2 Some groups support people who have a common need or interest e.g. residents associations and sports clubs.

3 Some voluntary organisations are pressure groups too e.g. the RSPB (Royal Society for the Protection of Birds) campaigns on environmental issues as well as running nature reserves.

4 Some provide a service e.g. the National Trust.

 PROJECT WORK

1 Follow a local campaign in the press or radio. Record what methods people use to achieve their aims.

 Questions

1 'Trying to change things is a waste of time'. How far do you agree?

2 Are you a member of any voluntary groups? Why do you think so many people are members of voluntary groups?

Vote for Me!

KEY ISSUES
- How does a citizen participate in politics?
- Is apathy (lack of interest or activity among voters) good or bad for politics?

Which of the two accounts below do you think told the real story of the 2001 General Election? Check the table to find out.

A Landslide

- Another big success for Labour. Blair back as PM.
- Conservatives did badly. Leader William Hague resigned.
- Liberal Democrats increased their vote from 1997 and gained six more seats.
- Only a few seats changed hands.

Apathy Rules OK

- The Labour Party won but with only 42% of the vote (lowest share of a winning party for 100 years).
- 17 million voters did not bother to vote.
- The turnout (the people who actually voted compared to those registered) nationally was only 59.3%.
- The Royal Society for the Protection of Birds now has more members than all the UK political parties combined!

Why Bother?

Politics and government is about power. People over 18 can vote and so choose the political party they want to win. Winning an election gives your party the authority (or mandate as it is known) to put the policies you agree with into practice.

Before a General Election, parties publish a manifesto – what they promise to do about issues like education, health and the economy.

Parliament makes the law in the United Kingdom. But the UK has signed treaties to agree that sometimes, the laws of the European Union will override UK laws.

In a democracy like the UK, people who are aged 18 and over can, through the use of their vote in a General Election, change the government.

▲ The centre of power in the UK?

▼ The results for the 2001 General Election (excludes Northern Ireland).

	Number of MPs	Net Gains/Losses	Total Vote	% of Vote	Change since 1997
Labour	412	−6	10.7m	42.0	−2.4
Conservative	166	+1	8.4m	32.7	+1.2
Liberal Democrat	52	+6	4.8m	18.8	+1.6
SNP	5	−1	0.46m	1.8	−0.2
PC	4	0	0.19m	0.8	+0.2
Others	12	0	–	–	–
Turnout	25,558,424 (59.3%)				
Swing	1.8% Labour to Conservative				

INFO BOX

TURNOUT

In Australia voting is compulsory. You **must** vote or pay a fine if you don't. Turnout is high. Australians say:

'People fought for the right to vote. If people don't vote they might lose their right to have a say. To be a proper democracy citizens must take part. Find out what the politicians are standing for. If you don't vote you have no right to complain about what politicians do in your name later. If you don't like the Government, vote it out!'

In this country you do not have to vote. In 2001 fewer people 'turned out' to vote in the General Election than ever before. The non-voters say:

'I'm not interested in politics. It's a waste of time. I can't make a difference. The political parties are all the same. Round here you know who is going to win so it doesn't matter if I vote or not.'

'Politicians are only interested in us when there is an election. I'd rather let the politicians get on with it.'

What do you think? Discuss with others:

'A citizen ought to vote'

Or

'It doesn't really matter if people don't vote. Apathy rules OK. '

Already the government has made it easier for people to apply for postal votes; they have experimented with longer voting hours, and are considering using supermarkets as polling stations as well as using emails, the internet and texting.

GLOSSARY

Elections: How electors vote in secret to choose someone to represent them on local councils (councillors), National and Regional Assemblies, Parliament (MPs) or the European Parliament (MEPs). In the UK elections are held on Thursdays.

Parliament: The two bodies which make the law for the UK; the House of Commons and the House of Lords. Meets at the Palace of Westminster in London.

Political parties: In Britain the three major parties are the Labour Party, the Conservative and Unionist Party (Tories) and the Liberal Democrat Party.

? Questions

1 How do you think more people could be encouraged to vote?
2 What is the case for and against lowering the voting age to 16 from the present age of 18?

▲ Tony Blair and Iain Duncan Smith speak at Prime Minister's Question Time.

Vote for Me!

Vote for Me!

Citizens Who Have Made a Difference

Martin Bell

Martin Bell, a BBC reporter, decided to stand as an Independent candidate in the 1997 General Election against Neil Hamilton. This former Conservative minister had been accused of accepting money from a businessman. Normally it is difficult for independent candidates to win because they don't have the help of a Party.

But Martin Bell won, although it had been a 'safe' Tory seat, He represented Tatton as MP until 2001.

▲ Martin Bell faces Neil Hamilton during the 1997 election campaign.

Dr Richard Taylor

Dr Richard Taylor was leader of a campaign group fighting to save Kidderminster Hospital. The group had already won 19 seats on the local council when Dr Taylor decided to stand in the 2001 General Election. He was elected by a large majority and beat a member of the Labour government.

Which evidence in the table shows you that:

- Richard Taylor gained votes from both the Labour and the Conservative parties?
- The Liberal Democrats decided not to fight for the seat?
- More voters stayed at home than in the previous election?

What Is All This Voting For?

General Elections

In a General Election each constituency elects one MP. The party that wins a majority of the seats forms the government.

Each constituency has, on average, 65,000 electors.

In Britain the **Prime Minister** decides when to call a General Election. It must be called within five years of the previous election. When an individual Member of Parliament dies or resigns a **by-election** is held.

Local Elections

Local elections are normally held in May on a date fixed by parliament. Some local authorities are all elected at the same time. Others put one-third of their wards into the election each year. Voters choose councillors to represent them on local issues.

Regional Parliaments and Assemblies

In Scotland, Wales and Northern Ireland there is a new level of devolved government

Candidate	Number of votes cast	% of votes cast	Change since 1997 % increase or decrease
Richard Taylor Kidderminster Hospital	28,487	58.1%	
David Lock Labour	10,857	22.1%	−26.7%
Mark Simpson Conservative	9350	19.1%	−17.0%
Jim Millington UKIP	368	0.8%	+0.2
Majority	17,630	35.9%	
Turnout 68%, −7.3% since 1997			

– some of the powers from central government are now decided by elected Parliaments and Assemblies. These new bodies use proportional voting systems – the percentage of votes cast for a party equals the percentage of seats won.

London now has a Greater London Authority with a directly elected Mayor. All of these changes occurred after local voters were asked to say in a **referendum** whether or not they wanted them. There are proposals to set up regional assemblies in England too.

 INFO BOX

HOW WE VOTE – THE DIFFERENT SYSTEMS

General Elections You vote by putting X on a ballot paper next to the candidate you want. The candidate with the most votes wins the seat. They do not have to gain a majority of the votes cast, just one more vote than the candidate in second place. This system is called 'First Past the Post'.

Local Elections in most of the UK (except Northern Ireland) also use the 'First past the Post' voting system.

European Elections You vote by a vote by putting X against the party you want. The country is divided into large **constituencies**. Each elects seven or more MEPs (Members of European Parliament). The political party decides the order of its candidates on the ballot paper. The seats are awarded according to the percentage of votes a party receives. If the Conservatives won two seats, the first two candidates on their list would be elected; so the system is called the Regional List system. European Elections are held every four years. Each country votes on different days but across Europe the votes are all counted on the same Sunday.

GLOSSARY

By-election: An election within one individual scat.

Constituencies: The voting areas into which a country is split up.

Prime Minister: The head of government in the UK, appointed by the monarch.

Referendum (plural = referenda): An election where you vote Yes or No on a single issue. It can take place at a local, regional or national level. Some countries (like Switzerland) have lots of referenda. In the UK there have been referenda about the Good Friday Agreement (in Northern Ireland), Scottish and Welsh devolution, and the London Mayor and Assembly.

? Questions

1 Explain why Martin Bell and Richard Taylor won their seats.
2 Find out why some people and political parties think that the 'First Past the Post' System is unfair.
3 Which of these issues do you think are so important that they should be decided by a referendum? Explain why.
   - whether Britain changes to Euros instead of the pound
   - whether the death penalty should be brought back
   - whether your region wants a Regional Assembly.

Vote for Me!

KEY ISSUES

○ Why are there different types of government in the United Kingdom?
○ Who makes the decisions?

Serving the People

Government within the UK operates at several levels. Why is this?

You may be concerned about an abandoned car outside your house, but would you write to the Prime Minister to get it moved? No – because this is a local issue. You may be concerned about the ozone layer, but do you expect your local councillor to resolve this issue? No – this is a global issue. You want your national government to deal with its global partners to sort it out.

All of us are affected by government decisions and the services that the government provides, either at a local, regional or national level. To get real service from government it has to be at the appropriate level – so it can cope with the issue.

The UK National Government is based in Westminster. The Parliament there has 'sovereignty' – power over all other types of government within the UK.

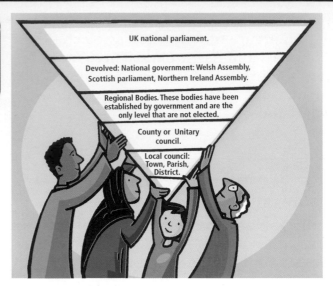

▲ The different levels of government in the UK.

Local government and devolved bodies have no automatic right to exist – they are set up by parliament and can be abolished or changed by parliament.

Local government has seen many changes. For example, now only a few councillors are responsible for running major services and are held accountable to all the councillors six or seven times a year. This is similar to how the cabinet works within central government.

Who Makes the Decisions at Each Level?

MPs At a General Election, we cast our votes to elect Members of Parliament (MPs). MPs receive a salary and allowances for employing staff and running their offices in

▲ Parliaments of Wales, Northern Ireland and the new Greater London Assembly building.

parliament and in their constituencies. Some MPs also have other jobs such as journalism or business. Ordinary backbench MPs debate and attend committees to decide how laws should be changed. After each General Election a new government is formed. Some MPs in the winning party are promoted to become Ministers or even Cabinet Ministers. Senior Cabinet ministers are called 'Secretary of State' e.g. Secretary of State for Northern Ireland. They run Departments and meet in **Cabinet** to make the important national decisions. Opposition MPs may become **Shadow spokespersons** – they oppose what the Government is doing. Frontbench MPs get extra salary.

Scottish Parliament and the Welsh and Northern Ireland Assembly members are full-time and receive an annual salary and allowances for staff.

Local Authority councillors are part-time and receive an annual allowance. Senior councillors, who are members of the cabinet, receive a larger allowance, because their positions take up a lot of time. A cabinet member responsible for the education service in your area could be responsible for an annual budget of £300 million and for many thousands of employees.

Town and parish councillors are unpaid and part-time.

GLOSSARY

Cabinet meetings: These regular meetings are chaired by the Prime Minister and make the important national decisions.

Shadow spokesperson: An MP from the major opposition party who speaks for their party on major issues and questions the government minister responsible for that area, e.g. Shadow Spokesperson for Health.

INFO BOX

COULD YOU STAND FOR ELECTION?

You need to be over 21 years old.

You can stand as an Independent.

But most people who stand for election are a member of one of the major political parties. You apply to be selected as a candidate. You get local people to nominate you.

You have to pay a deposit which you lose if you get under 5 per cent of the votes cast. This is to stop people doing it as a joke.

You then campaign in your ward or constituency. You are only allowed to spend a certain amount. For local elections it is a few hundred pounds. For a General Election it is several thousand pounds. However, the national parties spend tens of millions of pounds on national election campaigning. The assistance given by local Party members is extremely important to your chances of success.

Questions

The average local authority councillor is male, white, aged 55 and retired. Should local councillors be paid a salary like Members of Parliament? Would a salary help other representatives of the community (e.g. women, ethnic minorities, younger people) become councillors? Discuss your answers with a partner.

Prepare a speech to support one of these views:

Politicians have no experience of ordinary life. They do not understand people's problems. They need to stay in touch by having ordinary jobs and family lives as well as political ones.

or

Politicians need to be full-time to do the job properly. They shouldn't carry on their business interests or they might make decisions for the wrong reasons.

KEY ISSUES

○ Who has power in the UK?

The Monarchy

In Britain the Head of State is the King or Queen. In a republic, like the USA, the Head of State is a president who is elected. Over the years the monarchy has lost most of its power. Parliament and the Government actually rule.

The Prime Minister

The prime minister is the leader of the majority party in the House of Commons. The PM is appointed by the monarch and leads her government. A prime minister remains in power as long as they keep the support of their own party and/or parliament. Some British prime ministers have been accused of being presidential – having their own power – rather than working closely with Cabinet and Parliament.

The Cabinet

The Cabinet are the leading members of government. They are appointed by the prime minister, who can choose to replace them at any time. Each cabinet minister is responsible for running a major government department. The full cabinet meets once a week, but most of its business is done in smaller cabinet committee meetings.

Parliament

Parliament is the top law-making body within the UK. It is made up of the House of Commons and the House of Lords. Elected Members of Parliament sit in the House of Commons.

Parliament has two main powers:

1 To pass legislation – all MPs vote on proposed changes to the law.
2 Scrutiny – to hold the government, ministers and the prime minister accountable for their actions. MPs have the right to ask questions and to speak in debates.

Over the years, the power of parliament has seemed to decline and the power of the prime minister has appeared to increase.

The House of Lords is a second chamber. It has limited powers. It looks again at legislation that comes from the Commons and can amend it.

The House of Lords is changing. It used to be made up only of hereditary peers (those who have a title passed down from their parents or relatives). Some say it should consist only of **Life Peers** who are appointed because of their experience. Others say it should be elected. However an elected House of Lords would be a rival to the power of the House of Commons. An appointed body may not be able to stand up to the Government.

The European Union

Britain joined the European Union or EU in 1973. As a Member State Britain now shares some of its powers with the EU. Although the UK parliament makes laws, there are some areas that are governed by European Union law.

▲ Who has political power in the United Kingdom?

There are three structures which run the EU.

1 The Council of Ministers. Government ministers from each member country meet to make major decisions about the future of the EU.

2 The European Parliament has limited powers, but must be consulted on proposed changes to European law. Citizens throughout Europe elect its members (MEPs). It has the right to dismiss the European Commission.

3 The European Commission proposes policy for the EU. The president of the European Commission and the other European commissioners are chosen by the member governments. The UK has two commissioners.

INFO BOX

POWER OF THE EUROPEAN PARLIAMENT OVER THE EUROPEAN COMMISSION

All 20 EU Commissioners resigned in March 1999, following a report into fraud and favouritism. They knew that if they did not resign they would be sacked by the parliament. Some of the things uncovered included:

- A French commissioner appointed her dentist to a senior EU post.

- A Spanish commissioner acted slowly when fraud was discovered.

So Who Really Holds Power?

All of these bodies – parliament, the EU, national, regional and local government – have some power over our everyday lives. But maybe others have even more power and influence. Today we live in a global economy. Many believe that unelected **multinational companies**, the **mass media** and international financial organisations, such as the IMF (International Monetary Fund) and the WTO (World Trade Organisation) are the ones with the real power. Their economic control means that even national governments can't always make decisions about their own futures.

The European Union Debate

Currently the EU is a union of 15 countries (25 from 2004). Several former East European countries are due to join the EU. The EU aims to:

a) create a common economic market

b) develop political cooperation to ensure peace and democracy.

Some members wish to create a 'United States of Europe.' They believe this will allow Europe to balance the power of multinationals and the USA. Others want to keep the independence of the member states in a looser alliance.

What do you think is the best way forward?

GLOSSARY

Life Peers: Lords/Dames who are created in the 'Honours List' for service to public life and can sit for their lifetimes in the House of Lords.

Mass media: Methods of communicating with a large number of people at the same time, such as newspapers, magazines, radio, television, internet or interactive TV.

Multinational companies: Companies such as Coca Cola, Shell and Nissan which have worldwide operations and markets.

Questions

1 In the twenty-first century is there a need for a monarchy in the UK?

2 Do we need the EU to help control the power of multinationals?

KEY ISSUES

KEY ISSUES

○ The powers of protest – how far do they go?
○ Can people power make a difference?

Getting Involved

Elections only take place every four or five years. How can you make politicians listen to you in between elections?

On Your Board!

Paul and Jenny were keen skateboarders. But they were always getting moaned at for using the town centre. They decided to do something about it.

- They talked to other skateboarders and formed a group.
- The group organised a petition asking the council for a skateboard park.
- They convinced councillors of the need. They found part of a local public park that could be used.
- A few months later they got their photograph in the paper when the new skateboard park was opened.
- Peaceful protest had worked for them.

But what can you do when your country is not a democracy and bans free speech and protest?

▼ What means of protest do we have as individuals?

At School	In the Community
• Ask questions.	• Join local protest groups.
• Write letters.	• Petitions.
• Petitions.	• Contact local councillors or MPs/MEPs.
• School council.	
• Involve parents and governors.	• Involve the media.
	• Marches/protests.
• Discuss issues with the head teacher or principal.	• Join a political party.
• Involve the media.	

The Velvet Revolution

In November 1989 there was massive public protest against the **one-party**, communist system in former Czechoslovakia. The government fell and was replaced by a multi-party system. There was no violence and so this change became known as the 'Velvet Revolution'.

Vaclav Havel was elected as new president. He was a human rights **activist** who had been put in prison by the communists for speaking out.

In 1967 there had been a protest and the Russians had sent their army to crush it. But in 1989 the Russians did not send in the tanks. This allowed former Czechoslovakia and the other countries of Eastern Europe to end **communist** rule.

▲ Petition leads to skateboard park.

▲ People power – Prague 1989.

Nazi Germany

In Nazi Germany before the Second World War, democracy was replaced by a **totalitarian** state. People's freedoms were taken away. People were arrested or persecuted simply because of their religion or political ideas.

Pastor Martin Niemoller was put in a concentration camp for speaking out against the Nazis. He wrote this poem about people who kept quiet because they were afraid:

First they came for the Jews
And I did not speak out
Because I was not a Jew.
Then they came for the Communists
And I did not speak out
Because I was not a Communist
Then they came for the Trade Unionists
And I did not speak out
Because I was not a trade unionist.
Then they came for me
And there was no one left
To speak out for me.

Your Rights in the United Kingdom

In the UK we believe that the government should protect individual rights – freedom of speech, the right to protest and vote for the party we choose.

The European Convention of Human Rights is now part of UK law. This protects your rights in important areas: the right to a fair trial, freedom of thought and expression, right to free elections and the right to education.

What right to protest do you think a citizen should have? Think about where you stand on the following issues.

- *Strikes and picketing should always be legal.*
- *A National Front march should be able to march through whatever area it wants.*
- *Peaceful Sit down protests should always be allowed.*

INFO BOX

Should there be any limits on the right to protest? Governments say yes – some protests cause too much inconvenience or risk to others to be allowed. So in Britain all the following activities are, or have recently been, against the law:

- joining a trade union (at GCHQ, a defence agency).
- holding a rave party where you wish.
- holding a protest march where you wish.

- *Religious groups should be able to sing, chant or preach wherever and however they want.*
- *Roads and pavements should be closed off if there is a march.*

GLOSSARY

Activist: Someone who spends time openly working for political change.

Communists: Believe the state should control all land and factories, the Communist Party should control politics and that citizens of the state are equal.

One-party state: Where only one political party is allowed. There may be elections but there is only a choice between the candidates from one party.

Totalitarian state: The State is controlled by one political party and dominated by a strong leader. All power belongs to the state, e.g. Nazi Germany between 1933 and 1945.

Questions

1 Why did Pastor Martin Niemoller think he should take the risk of protesting against the Nazis?
2 Would you have spoken out if there were risks like those in Nazi Germany or Czechoslovakia?

Providing for our Needs as Citizens

Local and central government services affect us all every day.

Look at the circle.

Which local and community services do you already use?

Which national government services do you already use?

Which services do you think you will use more in the future?

Who Should Provide Public Services?

🗣 *'I think all these services should be run by the government and paid for out of our taxes. I believe in Nationalisation and public control.'*

🗣 *'I believe private companies run for profit make a better job of running public services. I believe in Privatisation.'*

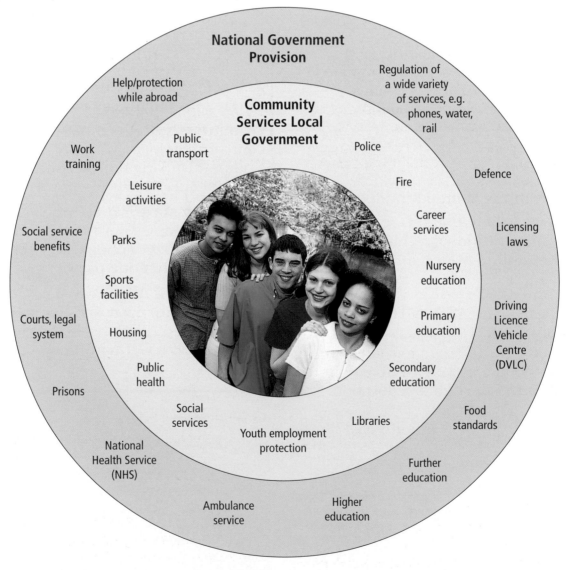

National Government Provision

Help/protection while abroad

Regulation of a wide variety of services, e.g. phones, water, rail

Community Services Local Government

Work training

Public transport

Police

Fire

Defence

Leisure activities

Career services

Licensing laws

Social service benefits

Parks

Nursery education

Sports facilities

Primary education

Driving Licence Vehicle Centre (DVLC)

Courts, legal system

Housing

Public health

Secondary education

Prisons

Social services

Libraries

Food standards

Youth employment protection

National Health Service (NHS)

Further education

Ambulance service

Higher education

▲ Services provided by government.

What do you believe?

In practice there is a mix of public and private control. There is still much argument about which services are best left completely public, and which should be run privately even though our taxes still pay for them.

Private companies run these essential services: water, gas, telephones and electricity. The government controls the quality of their services through regulators e.g. OFWAT (Office of the Water Industry Regulator).

Do you think the private companies do a good job? Is it right they make a profit out of services which are essential? (we cannot do without them).

Public/Private Partnerships

The Labour Government is encouraging public/private partnerships. This means private companies pay for the building of new hospitals, schools, motorways etc. Public money provided by hospital trusts, local councils or national government then pays them back each year for the use of the buildings.

Sometimes private companies directly manage the service as well.

Agencies

The government has converted some services into government agencies.

The Driving Licence Vehicle Centre (DVLC) in Swansea is typical. This agency manages its own affairs and budgets, but is still owned by the state and is accountable to government ministers.

- *'Clean Streets buys bigger better dust carts. They collect the rubbish faster.'*
- *'Clean Streets pays its staff less and doesn't give them holiday pay.'*
- *'Clean Streets makes its staff work harder. They can't knock off work early like they used to.'*
- *'Clean Streets only collects once a week and won't come back for bigger items or sweep up the mess.'*

INFO BOX

MAKING MONEY OUT OF RUBBISH

Many services that are controlled by local government have been opened up to private sector competition. All local councils have to place a wide range of their services out to tender. In many local areas the refuse collection is carried out by the private sector because local councils have to find the most cost-effective way of providing the service.

How does a private firm make money out of collecting our rubbish? If the local council spent £3.2 million a year to run its own service, and a private contractor 'Clean Streets' offered to run the same service for £2.7 million a year, the council would save its council taxpayers £500,000 a year. The council pays 'Clean Streets' the £2.7 million and the firm then has to provide the service and make a profit.

How do you think Clean Streets makes its profit?

CASE STUDY – THE RAILWAYS

Over recent years many people have complained about the state of the railways.

What do you think is the best way to improve the railway system?

'The State should re-nationalise and run the network for the whole country.'

'It should stay privatised – different companies should operate in different parts of the country. One company should own and maintain the track.'

'The State should step in to regulate the private companies and make sure they improve the services.'

How is My Life Affected?

Picking Up The Bill

Getting the Money

The Government can't provide services like health or education unless it raises money. It can do this by taxing us and by borrowing. The Chancellor of the Exchequer is in charge of this spending and borrowing and sets a Budget every year.

Government spending might have to go up for various reasons:

- to improve the National Health Service
- to pay for more police
- to pay for a war
- to pay for unemployment benefit if there is a recession (when the economy stops growing and people lose their jobs).

Look at the first pie chart to see what the Government spends our money on.

Money borrowed has to be paid back so governments try not to get into too much debt. So they use taxes. The Inland Revenue collects these. Look at the second pie chart to see how much is raised by each sort of tax.

How do we pay?

Through direct tax

Income Tax and National Insurance are taken directly from every employed person's wage. The more you earn the more you pay. This is why many think they are fairer. But you have no choice over paying this tax. People sometimes complain the government is spending most of the money on services which benefit poorer people.

Through indirect tax

- Value Added Tax (VAT) is paid when we buy anything. A percentage goes to the Government. If we don't buy much we don't pay much. But poorer people tend to pay higher taxes this way – because they have to buy things. Everyone pays whatever their income.

- Excise Duties are an extra tax on certain items such as fuel, alcohol, cigarettes and road fund licences (paid each year to keep people's cars on the road).

- Through taxes on business. Business Rates, Corporation Tax and Employers' National Insurance are paid direct to government. Firms pass on these costs through higher prices.

Through local tax

Council Tax is the local tax paid to councils based on the value of your property. This replaced the Community Charge (Poll Tax) in 1990. Poll tax (a flat rate per adult) had

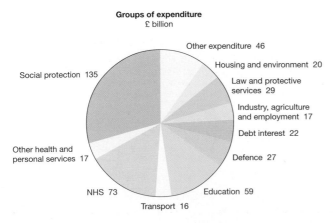

Groups of expenditure
£ billion

Other expenditure 46
Housing and environment 20
Law and protective services 29
Industry, agriculture and employment 17
Debt interest 22
Defence 27
Education 59
Transport 16
NHS 73
Other health and personal services 17
Social protection 135

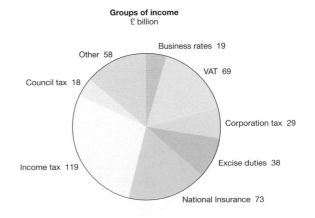

Groups of income
£ billion

Other 58
Business rates 19
VAT 69
Corporation tax 29
Excise duties 38
National Insurance 73
Income tax 119
Council tax 18

▲ Figures taken from HM Treasury, 2003/04.

been so unpopular it helped bring down Margaret Thatcher as Prime Minister. There had been non-payment protests, demonstrations and violent riots.

When asked, many people claim they wouldn't mind paying more tax to improve services like health. But in the UK and around the world political parties have often lost votes when taxes have gone up. In recent years the proportion of income paid in indirect tax has risen compared to direct tax. People get more in their wage packet but pay tax when they spend it.

▲ Angry farmers and hauliers protesting about the price of fuel in 2000.

INFO BOX

FUEL PROTESTS 2000

In 2000 the Government had a policy of raising fuel duty more than inflation (the rate of price increases each year). It saw this as a 'green tax' – if petrol was expensive people would use public transport more and their cars less. This would help the environment because cars and lorries cause pollution and greenhouse gases.

But oil companies put up their prices at the same time. Fuel cost more than it had ever done before.

Farmers were very angry. Their incomes were dropping because of other factors. They said this extra cost would break them.

Hauliers (lorry companies) were also angry. They had to compete with European hauliers who paid less for their fuel. They said this extra cost would bankrupt them.

In September 2000 some farmers and hauliers started blockading the oil refineries with their lorries and tractors. Other oil tanker drivers refused to cross their picket lines. Deliveries to garages stopped and motorists soon started running out of fuel.

The country was in danger of shutting down if essential workers such as nurses couldn't get to work. At first there had been a lot of public support for the protest because drivers didn't like paying the fuel duty either. But the government was forced to act once lives were put at risk.

The Government held indirect talks with protest leaders. It said it would look again at the way the fuel tax operated. The protesters knew they were losing public support. Within a few days the protest was over. Later when the protesters tried to restart the protest they did not succeed.

Questions

1 Would you be prepared to pay more direct tax to improve services like health?
2 Would you vote for a party which wanted to cut taxes?

The Long Arm of the Law

KEY ISSUES

○ Why do we need laws?
○ How are laws made?

Why We Need Laws

We need laws because:

- People need to know what is unacceptable behaviour.
- People need justice.
- Society needs to control its citizens. Otherwise people would selfishly do as they please. There would be anarchy (a complete lack of law and order). Then the strong and violent survive but the weak suffer.

A Just Legal System

Imagine that you are that little person in the cartoon below. You are using your new mobile phone, and the bully corners you and threatens you with violence unless you give them your phone. Nowadays we would expect help from the legal system against bullies like that. We would expect a just legal system to:

- encourage those around to show concern and offer help;
- encourage someone to call the police and offer to be a witness/identify the criminal;
- Provide a police force to gather evidence and to catch the criminal;
- Provide a court system so there was a trial;
- Provide a 'punishment to fit the crime' if found guilty.

INFO BOX

In 2002, a senior judge suggested that those who steal mobile phones in street robberies should receive long prison sentences. Many young people are victims of this crime. It is usually other young people who carry out this crime. Recently a young girl was shot in the head, just to steal her mobile phone from her.

▌▌ Do you think tougher sentences are the answer to mobile phone theft?

Every society has a legal system.

There are three parts to the legal system: law, police and courts; each is necessary to make sure justice is seen to be done.

- **Without courts:** You could be arrested but not found guilty and punished.
- **Without Laws:** The police could arrest you for anything they want, and the court could punish you in any way it wanted.
- **Without Police:** People would break the law but nobody would catch them, collect evidence or charge them. There would be nothing for the courts to do.

Who Makes the Law?

In the UK Parliament is the legislature (makes the laws).

A proposal for a new law is called a Bill. A Bill goes through several stages (or readings) in the Houses of Commons and Lords, before receiving the Royal Assent and becoming a law.

1 First reading. The Bill is read out loud, and 'Tabled' (put on the table).

2 Second reading. MPs discuss the major ideas behind the Bill. MPs vote on it. MPs can suggest amendments (changes).

3 If most MPs vote in favour the Bill goes to the Committee stage. A committee of MPs from different parties discusses the Bill in detail and proposes changes.

4 Report stage. The House of Commons considers the proposed changes and can make further changes.

5 Third reading. The Bill is discussed and MPs vote. If there is a majority in favour...

6 The same procedure is followed in the House of Lords. The Lords can amend or reject legislation, but it can only delay some Bills for one year.

7 Once through the House of Lords the Bill with the Lords's amendments has to go back to the Commons.

8 Once accepted, the Bill gets the Royal Assent (the Queen signs it) and becomes an Act of Parliament: the Law.

Case Study

Sometimes international law can help a UK citizen even when UK law doesn't. Caning in schools was banned when a mother won her case at the European Court of Human Rights.

In many areas of our life new laws are made by the European Union. If they conflict with UK law, EU law 'takes precedence' (comes first). An example is the new right for men to have 'paternity leave' (time off work to help with their newborn baby).

GLOSSARY

Punishment to fit the crime:
Punishments should match how serious the offence was.

Questions

1 Many groups have sets of rules to help them govern themselves. Can you think of any?

2 Design a new set of school or college rules for students. What would you include? Who would you consult? Who do you think should agree to them before they could be passed?

The Long Arm of the Law

KEY ISSUES

○ What is the difference between criminal and civil law?
○ How do the courts deal with criminal and civil cases?

Spot the Difference!

Criminal law is used when someone has committed a crime. Crime is anti-social. The police can arrest people who break criminal law. The state prosecutes the accused. (The Queen versus .....).

Civil law is used when there is a dispute between individuals or groups, often about property. The courts award damages (a money pay-out) or force someone to change their behaviour, e.g. not to see someone or visit them. The police aren't involved.

Is it Criminal or is it Civil?

THEFT	PERJURY	FORGERY	ROBBERY
POSSESSION OF DRUGS		MURDER	
ARGUMENT OVER A WILL		SPEEDING	
BANKRUPTCY	DIVORCE	DEBTS	

Criminal Cases

1 Police gather evidence against an individual.
2 The Crown Prosecution Service (CPS) decides if there is enough evidence to take the case to court.
3 The CPS prosecutes in court – puts forward the case against the accused.

Magistrate's Courts

Less serious criminal cases are dealt with by Magistrate's Courts. The decision about your guilt or innocence is made by three lay magistrates (part-time volunteers with no legal background). Magistrates can only impose limited sentences – maximum fine £5000 and/or 6 months in prison.

A Magistrate's Court is also the first hearing of serious cases such as murder. The Magistrates decide whether there is enough evidence for the case to proceed to a Crown Court for a full hearing. Magistrate's Courts also deal with licensing laws for pubs and casinos.

If Magistrates find you guilty, you can appeal to the Crown Court.

Some people prefer to have their case heard by the Crown Court because they think they would have a better chance with a jury trial.

Crown Courts

Serious crimes are tried in Crown Courts. If the accused pleads not guilty, the jury of 12 hears the evidence and reaches a verdict (guilty or not guilty). The judge sums up the evidence for the jury (see page 19) and provides legal guidance. Recorders (part-time judges) hear less serious cases. Serious cases are heard in front of Circuit Judges who are full-time, and the most serious cases are heard in front of a High Court Judge. Judges decide the sentence and can give a large fine or longer sentences. A famous Crown Court is the Old Bailey in London.

Civil Cases

1 **Small Claims Courts.** If your dispute involves claiming a small amount of damages, your case is heard in the Small Claims Court. Individuals are offered help and advice by court officials and often present their own case. This makes it cheap and accessible.
2 **The County Court** hears disputes about larger sums of money, repossession of homes, disputes between landlord and tenant, divorce matters and cases involving disputed wills and legacies. A District or Circuit Judge sitting alone decides these cases.
3 **The High Court.** The next stage of civil courts is the High Court. This consists of three separate divisions:

Queens Bench Division	Family Division	Chancery Division
Deals with cases referred by County Court, either due to amount of money involved or on a point of law.	Deals with all matters relating to families and personal relationships.	Deals with tax issues and disputes over wills and large complex financial disputes.

Appeals go to the Civil Division of the Court of Appeal.
Decisions by this court set the way that similar cases are dealt with in the future.

House of Lords
The Law Lords deal with criminal and civil cases referred by the Court of Appeal.
Cases are normally heard by five Law Lords. (Law Lords are senior judges who are made Life Peers.)

Still Think They Got It Wrong?

A convicted person can appeal from the Crown Court to the Criminal Division of the Court of Appeal, and then with the permission of the Court of Appeal, to the House of Lords.

If none of these appeals has worked but new evidence is available, a case can go to the Criminal Cases Review Commission (CCRC) who have the power to refer the case back to the Court of Appeal. Judges hear cases in the Court of Appeal and the House of Lords; no juries are involved.

◀ The Scales of Justice on top of the Old Bailey, London.

? Questions

1 'Jurors can't deal with some complex cases. Some decisions are better left to judges.' Debate whether jury trials are always the best idea.
2 Which of the following skills and personal qualities do you think are most important in a lay magistrate?
charm, ability to understand people from all walks of life, intelligence, sympathy for victims, spotting liars, good listener, experience, being male/female/black/white/young/old
3 'Frightening and complicated.' How do you think the legal system could be made more accessible to ordinary people? Think about victims, witnesses and defendants.

GLOSSARY

Jury: 12 citizens chosen at random to hear evidence and decide whether someone is guilty or not.

Protecting our Rights from Outside the UK

KEY ISSUES

○ How can disputes be settled using European law or other methods?

There are two important courts outside the UK available to UK citizens.

1 European Court of Justice

Judges from the member states of the EU settle matters of dispute between member states. Both individuals and organisations can take cases to the court, providing they deal with issues relating to the European Union.

The Court can impose very large fines. The French government was fined millions of pounds a day when it broke EU law by refusing to import British beef following the BSE outbreak in Britain.

2 European Court of Human Rights

This Court in Strasbourg was set up as a result of the European Convention of Human Rights. This was an agreement between all the countries of Europe, not just the EU. This convention laid down basic human rights. The UK made it part of UK law by passing the Human Rights Act in 1998. Before this,

▲ The European Court of Human Rights in Strasbourg.

individual British citizens had to appeal directly to the Court when British courts had not supported them. Over the course of 30 years the Court said the UK government had broken the convention over 50 times.

The Human Rights Act affects us all. Now, UK courts can decide human rights cases. The Court in Strasbourg is still the last court of appeal.

Other Ways of Settling Disputes

The courts are often expensive, waste time and frighten people. You don't have to use the courts.

ⓘ INFO BOX

WHAT OPTIONS ARE AVAILABLE TO YOU TO SETTLE A DISPUTE?

- Direct negotiation with the other person.
- Mediation: using a third party to seek agreement – someone that each side agrees to.
- Ombudsman: an external and independent investigator (e.g. local government ombudsman) or set up by a specific industry (e.g. financial services ombudsman).
- Regulators: established by the government to safeguard consumer interests (e.g. Gas, Water and Electricity).
- Arbitration: a neutral 'referee' considers both sides' evidence and makes a decision which is binding.
- Tribunals: e.g. Industrial Tribunal. A legally qualified chairperson hears evidence from employers and employees/ trade unions. They fix compensation. Their decisions are binding. Other tribunals deal with issues such as taxes and social security.

The European Convention Of Human Rights

This covers the following.

- The state cannot take someone's life (except in limited circumstances).
- You cannot be tortured or treated in an 'inhumane or degrading way'.
- You cannot be treated as a slave.
- Clear legal procedures must be followed regarding arrest and detention.
- You have the right to a public, fair trial within a reasonable time. In criminal cases you are presumed innocent until proved guilty.
- You have the right to a private and family life – respect for your privacy, your home and family.
- You are free to hold a broad range of views and religious belief.
- You have the right to hold opinions and express your views.

- You have the right to assemble (meet) with others in a peaceful way. Also the right to associate with others, e.g. to form a trade union.
- You have the right to marry. Men and women have the right to marry and start a family. National laws can still govern how and at what age.
- You have the right to the peaceful enjoyment of your property.
- You have the right to education.
- You have the right to free and fair elections by secret ballot.
- Abolition of the death penalty. The death penalty can only be used in very exceptional circumstances, e.g. war.
- No discrimination. You have the right not to be treated differently on grounds of race, religion, sex, political views or any other status.

▲ Ballot boxes ensure that a person's vote remains secret.

? Questions

1 Explain each of the points above in your own words.
2 Think of five issues you think are likely to come before the courts concerning these rights. (Look out for them in the news).

Case Studies

The Law in Action

One of your responsibilities as a citizen is serving on a jury. With 11 other citizens chosen at random you have to decide the verdict in a court case. Citizens must also report a crime and serve as a witness if asked.

▲ How could you be involved?

Case Study – A Mugging

Darinda and her mother are out shopping when Darinda meets some friends. Suddenly a man approaches the group. He punches Darinda's friend Alesha, steals her mobile phone, and runs off. Alesha is upset but unhurt.

Alesha calls the police who quickly arrive. They take statements from Darinda, her friends and her mother. The group are able to give a good description of the man who stole the phone.

A week later Alesha is asked to visit the police station and agrees to look at an identity parade. She identifies the man who stole her phone. The police charge him with robbery and send all their evidence to the Crown Prosecution Service.

Then the Magistrate's Court holds a committal hearing. Three magistrates hear the case. They are advised by the **Clerk to the Justices**. The press report the case in the local paper.

Because the offence was serious, the magistrates send the **defendant** to the Crown Court for trial. The defendant is unemployed so he receives **Legal Aid** to pay for his defence. The magistrates have the power to remand someone in custody (keep him in prison) if they feel he will commit further crimes. Or they can release him on bail until the Crown Court trial.

The defendant pleads not guilty to the offence and so a full jury trial takes place at the Crown Court. Alesha sits anxiously in the witness's waiting room before giving evidence.

1 First the **barrister** for the Crown outlines the prosecution case. Witnesses are called to give evidence to support the case

▲ A Magistrate's court.

▲ A Crown Court case.

against the accused. Alesha tells the Court about the robbery. The Crown barrister carefully leads her through her evidence, asking her if she recognises the person who attacked her in court. Alesha points to the defendant.

2 The judge invites the barrister for the defence to cross-examine (question) Alesha. This barrister challenges her evidence, especially her original description of the robber. Darinda and her mother are called as witnesses and are cross-examined. The defendant's barrister calls witnesses to support the defendant's claim that he has an alibi (was elsewhere at the time of the offence). These witnesses are cross-examined by the Crown's barrister.

3 After all the witnesses are called, both the prosecution and the defence make closing statements to the court.

4 The judge sums up the evidence. He points out to the jury the main points of law involved and which parts of the evidence need to be closely examined.

5 The jury retire to consider their verdict. In the jury room they sit and discuss the evidence. The foreperson of the jury asks for people's verdicts – guilty or not guilty. If they do not all agree, they will discuss the matter further. In this case the jury cannot reach a unanimous verdict (one which they

all agree on). The court meets again and the judge agrees to accept a majority verdict, a maximum of 10 votes to 2. The jury retire and reach a majority verdict.

The court meets again and the jury have decided by 10 votes to 2 that the defendant is guilty.

6 The judge passes a sentence, bearing in mind any previous convictions of the accused and any 'mitigating factors' (which help lessen the sentence). In this case the defendant had previous convictions for robbery and was sentenced to 12 months in prison.

7 Any appeal against a Crown Court decision goes to the Court of Appeal (see pages 54–55). Appeal cases are heard before at least two High Court judges and do not involve juries.

GLOSSARY

Barrister: A highly qualified lawyer who represents clients in the Crown Court. (Solicitors represent clients in the Magistrates Court).

Clerk to the Justices: A legally qualified full-time court official who provides legal advice to magistrates.

Defendant: The person accused of the crime.

Legal Aid: Taxpayers' money which pays for the defence team if the defendant is poor.

? Questions

1 Give each stage of the case study a suitable title.
2 Look at the picture of a Magistrates Court. Identify the magistrates, the Clerk to the Justices, the defendant, the press, the defence solicitor, the public gallery.
3 Look at the picture of a Crown Court. Identify the Judge, the jury, the defendant, and press gallery.

KEY ISSUES

○ Do we have a right to privacy?
○ What rights do young people have?

The Case of the Killers of James Bulger

▲ James disappearing from the shopping centre, caught on CCTV.

Bulger Killers Win Freedom

In June 2001, Jon Venables and Robert Thompson, aged 18, were freed on Life Licences, having spent eight years in secure accommodation for the murder in 1993 of two-year-old James Bulger.

Background

February 1993
James Bulger, aged two, was abducted from a shopping centre in Bootle. James's battered body was found near a railway line. CCTV footage from the shopping centre led the police to arrest Thompson and Venables. As they were both aged ten, their names were not allowed to be released to the press or the public.

November 1993
Thompson and Venables, aged ten, were convicted of James Bulger's murder and (unusually) named by the judge. Their sentence was at least eight years in **secure youth accommodation**.

December 1999
The European Court of Human Rights (ECHR) decided that Thompson and Venables did not receive a fair trial. The court set up had not respected their rights as children. They had not been questioned fairly.

26 October 2000
The **Lord Chief Justice** ruled that the **parole process** for Thompson and Venables could begin. There was public protest, especially in Merseyside. They could soon be free.

Here's what different people said about their rights:

- *'The two boys had been only ten. They didn't really understand what they were doing.'*
- *'In many countries they wouldn't have been put on trial like that. They would have had a children's hearing.'*
- *'Eight years was a fair sentence because time passes so slowly for children.'*
- *'The sentence worked. They were rehabilitated (changed for the better).'*
- *'They were no longer a danger. They had served their punishment'*

'Ten-year-olds should know right from wrong.'
'The public wanted a proper trial reported by the press.'
'The sentence may not have worked. How can you tell?'
'Eight years was too little. They couldn't be punished enough for what they did.'
'The victim's family still wanted retribution (to make the boys suffer more and so pay back for the pain they had caused)'

A Right to Privacy?

Thompson and Venables's names were known so they were given new secret identities for their own protection. An **injunction** banned anyone from giving out details of their new lives. This was to protect their 'lives and physical safety.' In June 2001 they were released.

◀ An angry crowd protest outside the Court as Venables and Thompson are driven away.

But the same month, the Manchester Evening News published information about where they were. The **Attorney General** took the MEN to court for breaking the injunction.

The Family Division of the High Court heard the case. The case involved the rights of Thompson and Venables to have their confidentiality protected under the Human Rights Act 1998. Both sides were represented by barristers and called witnesses to support their case. The judge alone decided the outcome. There was no jury present. The judge ruled that the boys' right to confidentiality was more important than the right of the media to publish information about them. In this case the newspaper was fined £30,000 for contempt of court. It could consider an appeal to the House of Lords.

GLOSSARY

Attorney General: Senior government law officer.

Injunction: A binding legal direction prohibiting certain actions.

Life Licence: Anyone who has committed murder is only released on licence. If they break their conditions they are sent straight back to prison.

Lord Chief Justice: The most senior judge in England and Wales. Scotland and Northern Ireland have their own Lord Chief Justice.

Parole process: Preparing someone for release on licence.

Secure youth accommodation: Run by local councils. Where the most serious young offenders are locked up.

? Questions

Discuss both sides of the argument to the following questions.

1. Should Thompson and Venables have a right to privacy?
2. Are children fully responsible for their crimes? Do they deserve to be punished like adults?
3. Should prison be mainly for rehabilitation or punishment (retribution)?
4. Should the victim/victim's family have a say in the length of punishment given?

KEY ISSUES

○ What can you do if the legal system lets you down?
○ How can public and media pressure help?

The Case of Stephen Lawrence

▲ Stephen Lawrence.

April 1993
Stephen Lawrence, an 18-year-old sixth form student, and his friend Duwayne Brooks were rushing to catch a bus. They were set upon by a gang of four to six white youths. Duwayne was chased off. Stephen was stabbed. He staggered 200 metres and then collapsed in a pool of blood and died. The murder was racist.

Why Is This Case So Different?
The murder of Stephen Lawrence led to two police inquiries and the Stephen Lawrence Report. No-one has been successfully prosecuted for his murder. His killers still walk free. Stephen's family feel they have not got justice. Why is this?

Were certain people in the police and the Crown Prosecution Service (CPS) incompetent? (bad at their job)

Were mistakes made because certain people were racist and didn't investigate properly because Stephen was black?

Was the whole legal system racist?

Has the system now improved? Can black people get justice?

What Did the Police Do?
The police received many tip-offs within hours of the murder. But they did not follow these up or interview suspects quickly. Important **forensic evidence** like weapons and blood stains was probably lost.

The police later admitted that they had enough evidence to arrest two out of their five suspects, but they decided to wait. The police kept a watch on the suspects' homes, but did not follow them when they went out because they did not have mobile phones to call for back up.

Two youths aged 16 and 17 were charged with murder but later released after the CPS said there was a lack of evidence.

So the Lawrence family complained about the police investigation.

The police held two internal inquiries. They investigated themselves. Both said there had been no problems and no mistakes made.

Private Prosecution 1996
The family brought a private prosecution against the other three suspects because the CPS would not prosecute. The jury viewed evidence which showed the accused using aggressive and racist language. The accused kept refusing to answer questions in court saying, 'I claim the right to remain silent.' But the judge directed the jury to acquit the three because the prosecution evidence was not strong enough. As the law stands they cannot now be prosecuted for Stephen's murder (the Double Jeopardy rule).

Still no justice?
Many people were shocked that the five suspects were still free. There was fear of violent protest unless the issues were tackled. Stephen's family now had the backing of a

campaign. The media started to back them. Stephen's parents were interviewed by the papers. Nelson Mandela met them and sympathised. In 1997, the Daily Mail devoted its front page to Stephen's case. Under the headline 'Murderers', it published the pictures of the five suspects. The Mail invited the five to sue for libel. They have not yet taken up the offer.

Some congratulated the Mail for stepping in where the law had clearly failed; others called it 'Trial by Media'.

The Stephen Lawrence Report

The Government appointed an ex-High Court Judge to investigate what had gone wrong. In 1998 there were 68 days of public hearings. The five accused were pelted with missiles by the crowd outside. The five showed contempt for the hearing with answers like, 'I can't remember,' and 'I've no idea.'

The Report said:

- The Metropolitan Police were '**institutionally racist**'. Police forces must tackle the crisis of confidence between themselves and the black community.
- The Race Relations Act should be extended to cover the police, the armed forces and the Immigration Service (it didn't before).
- Victims should be given more details of evidence before trials.
- Using racist language should be made a criminal offence.
- Schools should teach the value of cultural diversity.

The Metropolitan Police have now made race crime a priority and set up a Racial and Violent Crime Task Force. This is trying to collect new evidence on Stephen's murder.

GLOSSARY

Forensic evidence: Scientific evidence that can be used to prove a suspect was involved e.g. blood, fingerprints.

Institutional Racism: A collective failure by an organisation to tackle racism.

? Questions

Never again? Do you think the case has brought a better determination to stamp out racism at all levels in society? Who do you agree with? Give reasons for your answers.

'It brings in a new era of race relations.' Tony Blair

'A lot of good has come out of it but we have to make sure this doesn't happen again.' Stephen's father

'Black lives are cheap.' Nelson Mandela to Stephen's family.

'The police have lost so much time. Unless they (the five) confess, it will take a miracle to get enough evidence to convict them.' Doreen Lawrence on the 10th anniversary of her son's death.

▲ Three of the murder suspects leave the Stephen Lawrence Inquiry.

How Does the Law Affect Me?

The Right to Live or Die

KEY ISSUES

○ Should courts decide life or death issues?
○ Human rights – how are they defined?

Case One

Miss B was a 43-year-old woman who could not move or breathe without the aid of a life-support machine. But she was fully conscious and able to speak.

She wanted to die and asked her doctors to turn the machine off. They refused because they believed it their duty to save life. So she applied to the High Court to request that her life-support machine be switched off.

Miss B gave evidence to the judge from her hospital bed. Miss B explained that she was aware of the consequences of having her life-support machine switched off, and said '*I want to be able to die.*' The judge said that the only issue for the court to decide was whether Miss B was able to make the decision to refuse further treatment.

Her chances of any improvement were less than 1 per cent. The doctors could not say what life would be like for her until a whole range of tests had taken place. She could have the use of a spinal jacket to support her back, a powered wheelchair

▲ Miss B's bedside.

or artificial arms controlled by her mouth or eyes.

In the past the High Court has allowed doctors to stop supporting the lives of people in a 'persistent vegetative state' (a coma) with no chance of recovery. This case was different because Miss B was mentally alert and able to communicate.

In her judgement, the judge said Miss B had the 'necessary mental capacity' to decide to refuse medical treatment. The judge gave Miss B the right to transfer to another hospital where her wishes would be carried out.

A few weeks later, Miss B died peacefully in her sleep after doctors at her new hospital switched off her life support machine.

 Do you think the judgement was correct?

Case Two

Diane Pretty was a 43-year-old mother of two who had Motor Neurone Disease. This disease is incurable and eventually causes paralysis of all muscles, and death when your breathing muscles became affected by the disease. Diane was already paralysed from the neck down and unable to talk without the aid of equipment. She wanted to end her life with dignity. (Suicide is legal). But she needed help from someone to assist her to die. Anyone assisting someone to die is committing a crime. Diane wanted her husband to assist her to die when she wished; but to protect her husband from criminal prosecution she applied to the courts.

She argued that under the Human Rights Act she had the right to die. This is because the Human Rights Act 'Prohibits Torture or Treatment that is Inhumane or Degrading' and gives 'The Right to Respect for Private and Family Life.'

But she lost a series of court cases.

She appealed to the House of Lords where her case was rejected.

She appealed to the European Court of Human Rights, who agreed to hear her case urgently. Diane was supported in her case by the pressure group **Liberty** and the **Voluntary Euthanasia** Society.

On 29 April 2002 the European Court of Human Rights rejected Diane Pretty's appeal. Under UK law **assisted suicide** is still illegal.

She died from the disease on 11 May 2002.

▲ Diane Pretty and her husband.

What do you think the Court should have decided?

GLOSSARY

Assisted suicide: When someone is too sick or disabled to independently kill themselves and asks for help from someone else.

Liberty: A UK-based pressure group that campaigns on human rights and justice issues.

Voluntary euthanasia: When someone consents to a doctor actively ending their life when the patient wants to die (e.g. by injection).

? Questions

1 How does Diane Pretty's case differ from that of Miss B?
2 Explain each case from the point of view of
   – the individual
   – the relatives
   – the doctors
   – the law.
3 Do you think Parliament should change the law and make
   a) assisted suicide legal?
   b) voluntary euthanasia legal? (allowing doctors to actively end life when the patient requests it)
   Give reasons for your answer.
4 What problems in society might there be if assisted suicide or voluntary euthanasia were made legal? Think about
   – the fears of elderly or sick people
   – pressures on relatives
   – pressures on doctors and nurses
   – greedy or uncaring relatives
   – religious and moral beliefs about death and murder.

Have I Got News for You?

When you buy a newspaper or switch on the TV in Britain you have a choice. But **non-democratic governments** do not have free media. They make sure the State controls the **mass media** because they know the power it has to influence people's opinions. The former Taliban government in Afghanistan controlled both newspaper and TV content. It banned the use of satellite dishes so that people could not get news from outside.

In this country we expect to have a **free press**. This means:

- there are lots of newspapers to choose between
- they report the truth
- they report a variety of opinions fairly
- they don't just say what the Government wants us to believe
- they cover important political events so we can make up our own minds about them
- they don't just say what their owners and advertisers want us to believe.

Is the press in Britain really free? Are our TV channels free of political bias?

Many people have concerns that our media isn't that free or that uses its power wrongly. They say:

- 🗣 *The press expresses the views of its owners – rich and powerful people.*
- 🗣 *The media is too powerful in influencing public opinion.*
- 🗣 *The media will say anything to boost circulation or viewers – even if untrue or unfair.*
- 🗣 *The media trivialises important issues –*
- 🗣 *celebrity takes over from real news.*
- 🗣 *The media sensationalises issues – using headlines and language to shock people.*
- 🗣 *The media hardly reports at all what happens in poorer parts of the world – so we don't know or care.*
- 🗣 *The media over-reports what happens in richer parts of the world especially the USA – so we don't get a true picture.*

▲ Is the media free and fair?

Case Study – The People's Princess

On 31 August 1997 Diana, Princess of Wales was killed in a car crash. Because Diana was divorced from the Prince of Wales, the rules stated she no longer had the title Her Royal Highness or was a member of the Royal Family. The newspapers said the monarchy did not care and were out of touch. The Prime Minister stepped in to work directly with the Palace, to improve its relations with the public. The Prime Minister coined the phrase the 'People's Princess', the flag at Buckingham Palace was lowered (against Royal rules) and the Queen met the public who had come to grieve. For the first time, the Queen spoke live to express her sorrow about the death of Diana. This was written in consultation with 10 Downing Street.

Television had a huge impact. On the day of her funeral more than 1 million people lined the streets of London, but an estimated 2.5 billion people worldwide watched live on TV.

▲ The death of Diana.

The Power of the Press – The Watergate Affair

US President Richard Nixon was forced to leave his office after the press investigated wrongdoing by his staff. In 1972, the Washington Post broke the story of a break-in at the Watergate building. Two reporters later found out that senior members of the Republican Party had ordered this burglary of the HQ of the Democratic Party, in the lead up to the Presidential Elections. Nixon's staff had hoped to find evidence that would damage the Democrats' chances. Nixon tried to cover up the story, but eventually he was forced to release audio tapes of conversations that proved that he knew what was happening. Nixon resigned in disgrace.

Gagging the Press – Thalidomide

In 1972, the Sunday Times wanted to print a story about the thousands of children offered poor compensation by the drug maker who had caused their deformities by not testing Thalidomide properly. Their mothers had taken this drug to stop morning sickness when they were pregnant. The Attorney General won an injunction that stopped the story being published. The House of Lords upheld this decision. The paper appealed to the European Human Rights Court which ruled against the Government. A new law to improve testing of new drugs was brought in.

PROJECT WORK

Look at a range of press and TV reports. Is there evidence to support people's concerns about the media?

GLOSSARY

Free press: When the press can publish information freely.

Mass media: Methods of communicating with a large number of people at the same time, such as newspapers, magazines, radio, television, internet or interactive TV.

Non-democratic governments: Where there are no free and fair elections/people have not chosen their rulers.

? Questions

1 Is TV news more reliable than news in the press? Explain your answers.
2 Why are politicians so concerned about their media image?

▲ Nixon resigns.

Is the Press too Powerful?

KEY ISSUES

○ Is the press too powerful?

Named, Shamed

In July 2000, the News of the World published a front page story headlined 'Named, Shamed'.

▲ Paedophiles were named and shamed.

This was a list of people whose names were on the Register of Sexual Offenders because they were said to be paedophiles.

Vigilante groups attacked those named and forced many to move home. Some people with similar names were also attacked.

The police complained the News of the World had made it more difficult to protect children. Police would prefer to know where these people are and keep an eye on them. They do not want them forced into hiding where they can't be traced.

The media had been reporting many stories about paedophiles (people who sexually desire children). It had given blanket coverage to the Sarah Payne case. She had been murdered by Roy Whiting, a man who had already served a prison sentence for kidnapping and serious sexual assault. The News of the World campaigned for harsher sentences and for parents to take the law into their own hands.

▲ Paedophile protest in Portsmouth 2000.

The Power to Influence – The Sun

Did you know that different newspapers support different political parties? Throughout the 1980s and early 1990s, a majority of the national press supported the Conservative Party. In 1992, The Sun declared 'It was the Sun wot won it' when John Major, the Conservative Prime Minister, unexpectedly won the General Election.

'It was the Sun wot won it'

On the day of the election, The Sun's front page attacked Labour leader Neil Kinnock:

By 1997 The Sun had changed sides and supported Tony Blair and the Labour Party. Labour won.

The Sun and other Murdoch-owned newspapers are very anti-EU. Should newspapers try to influence public opinion like this?

The Impact of the Press

Newspapers are printed during the night and front page stories can be changed quickly as events emerge. Radio and TV bulletins often pick up on stories run by the press. In the past the **quality (broadsheet) newspapers** were very influential. But more politicans now wish to get positive **tabloid (popular)** coverage.

Newspaper Sales	National Daily Tabloid Newspapers
Daily Mirror	1,955315
Daily Star	912,630
The Sun	3,521,427
Daily Express	910,034
The Daily Mail	2,348,723

Newspaper Sales	National Daily Broadsheet Newspapers
The Daily Telegraph	898,681
Financial Times	410,814
The Guardian	369,482
The Independent	179,427
The Times	594,353

Source: ABC (Audit Bureau of Circulation), July 2003.

PROJECT WORK

Compare a range of national daily newspapers.

- Sort them into tabloid (popular press) and broadsheet (quality press) sizes.
- Compare their treatment of news through language, photographs and headlines.
- What different audiences do they appeal to? How can you tell?
- Can you tell which (if any) political party the paper supports? Is it left wing, right wing or middle of the road?

GLOSSARY

Popular press/tabloid press: Mass circulation papers that contain a range of different types of news, sport and popular news stories. Often more entertainment than serious news. Usually cheaper than quality press.

Quality press/broadsheet newspapers: More serious news from the UK and abroad plus news relating to the business world. More expensive and contain more pages than tabloids.

Vigilantes: People who take the law into their own hands by attacking someone who has broken the law.

Questions

1 Discuss:

Was the News of the World right to 'name and shame'?

How far do you think newspapers influence the way people vote?

Which newspaper do you prefer for which kinds of news. Why?

Protection from the Media

> ### KEY ISSUES
> ○ Do citizens have a right to privacy?

Should the Press be Controlled?

UK tabloids publish many stories about the rich and famous. In the 1990s there were concerns that the press had gone too far intruding into their lives. The government threatened to introduce a privacy law to control the press. So the press decided to regulate itself and set up the Press Complaints Commission (PCC). This is made up of newspaper editors, public representatives and an independent chair. But many say the PCC 'lacks teeth'. It can only rule against a paper and make it apologise. It cannot fine newspapers. People who have enough money to sue sometimes prefer to use civil law to claim damages.

None of our Business?

Should newspapers just leave people alone to get on with their private lives? Or do the public have a right to know absolutely everything about celebrities?

Consider the following cases. Was the paper right or wrong to publish? Do you agree with the PCC/court decision?

Case One
The Daily Telegraph wrote that the Prime Minister's son, Euan Blair, was interviewed for a place at Oxford University. The Blairs complained. The PCC said the Telegraph was wrong to publish. Euan Blair is not a politician. The article was an 'unnecessary intrusion'. Where he wants to be a student is none of our business.

Case Two
The Sunday People published a set of nude photos of Sara Cox, a radio presenter, and her husband on honeymoon. The PCC told the paper's editor to apologise. Sara Cox decided that was not enough and sued under Article Eight of the Human Rights Act (which protects an individual's right to a private life). She received £50,000 in damages. The People and the photographic agent must pay costs of over £200,000.

Case Three
The Daily Mirror published a photograph showing Naomi Campbell leaving a meeting

> ### ⓘ INFO BOX
>
> **RIGHT TO PRIVACY**
>
> The Human Rights Act 1998 gave UK citizens the 'Right to Privacy'. Judges now have to interpret cases one by one according to this.
>
> But should the Government step in with a new law which defines privacy and how far the media can go?

▲ The right to privacy – Naomi Campbell.

▲ Sara Cox, DJ.

▲ Will Young.

of Narcotics Anonymous. (She had never admitted her drug problems to the papers.) She took the Mirror to court over its intrusion. Although she won her case she only got a small amount of damages. All the newspapers then wrote negative stories about her life.

Privacy Today?

The 'Pop Idol' competition attracted millions of viewers. More young people voted to decide the winner of the competition than voted in the 2001 General Election. Within weeks of winning, Will Young told reporters that 'media pressure' led him to talk about his private life and come out as gay: 'I don't wish to talk about it any further…my private life is my private life'.

Public Interest

The press often defends its stories by saying they are 'in the public interest'. This does not mean they are interesting! It means publishing the information brings such benefits to public life that it justifies any harm done to the individual.

The Case of Mary Bell

In 1972 Mary Bell, aged 11, was jailed for the murder of a 3-year-old boy. She suffered years of abuse in prison. She was released aged 23 and changed her name to start a

new life. She had a daughter who knew nothing about her mother's past. In 1998, the Sun found out where Mary lived and the press gathered outside her home. Mary's 14-year-old daughter then discovered about her mother's past. Within hours the family was forced into hiding.

ⓘ INFO BOX

COMPLAINING ABOUT THE PRESS

The Press Complaints Commission can only decide on issues that break its Code Of Conduct. Examples:

- Reports must be accurate.
- People should be given a fair opportunity to reply.
- No intrusion into people's private lives.
- No witness in a court case should be paid.
- The press must not harass.
- Children under 16 should not be interviewed or photographed without parental permission.
- Victims of crime should not be identified unless the law permits it.
- Confidential sources should be protected.

Newspapers are allowed to break the Code if the story is in the 'public interest'.

❓ Questions

1 Was it in the public interest to publish the following stories:
   – where the people who killed James Bulger are now living (see page 60)?
   – where Mary Bell is and her new name?
   Explain your answers.
2 Do famous people have enough protection from intrusive reporters?
3 Should newspapers regulate themselves through the Press Complaints Commission?

The Power of Television

KEY ISSUES

○ How powerful is television?
○ How does TV affect our lives?

If You Want the Truth, Turn on the TV?

Terrestrial TV channels such as BBC and ITV must not show **political bias**. They have 'charters' – rules that tell them to be neutral. Their news and documentaries should show both sides of an argument. News should not favour one party more than another. Most people trust television news to be fair and unbiased. Most people rely on it for their main news. Pictures and sound make more of an impact than just words. So it can influence our views more than the press.

Television can help change our attitudes for the good:

- When a BBC play called 'Cathy Come Home' was broadcast it shocked people by showing the problems of homelessness. A pressure group called 'Shelter' was formed to help. Shelter is still campaigning today.

- When Esther Rantzen campaigned about children in danger, a new organisation called 'ChildLine' was founded.

- When Michael Buerke did a special BBC news report on a famine in Ethiopia in 1984 Live Aid Concerts were set up that raised over £60 million.

◀ ChildLine helps young people in danger or distress.

ℹ INFO BOX

NUMBER OF HOURS OF TELEVISION VIEWING

Average Weekly Viewing per Person	
BBC1	5hr 42min
BBC2	2hr 31min
ITV	5hr 12min
Ch4	2hr 16min
Ch5	1hr 26min
Other	5hr 49min

Source: BARB (Broadcasters Audience Research Board), August 2003.

▲ South Park.

▲ Eastenders.

▲ ITN newscasters Dermot Murnaghan and Kirsty Young.

▲ Darren Campbell wins Gold.

▲ Live Aid Concert.

- Both BBC and ITV help to raise millions of pounds for charities through the Children in Need Appeal and Red Nose Day.

What the News Tells Us!

Most of us rely upon television for news from around the world. But does TV help us understand the background of the news story?

Consider these concerns:

- *'We mostly hear the views of white people who speak English.'*
- *'We see the grieving families of one side but only the angry street demonstrations of the other side.'*
- *'One side are shown as freedom fighters but the other side are shown as terrorists.'*
- *'The programmes assume you know how the problem started but I don't.'*
- *'What if no TV cameras are allowed in? Without pictures the country doesn't get on the news at all.'*

The story of the Arab/Israeli conflict was analysed by the Glasgow University Media Group. One young person explained how the news coverage affected him – the language and pictures were not neutral:

'You always think of the Palestinians as being really aggressive because of the stories you hear on the news. I always put the blame on them in my own head.'

INFO BOX

THE NEW MEDIA

The term for electronic technologies including satellite and digital television, radio and telephone and internet, interactive television, CD-ROM and streaming audio.

? Questions

1 Which has more power over our views on news issues – TV or the press?
2 Do we watch too much television? Does it influence too much of our thinking?
3 Can you trust information from the internet more or less than TV and newspapers? Explain your answer. Think about:
   - the charters of BBC and ITV requiring their news coverage to be neutral.
   - anyone, anywhere can set up their own website to say what they like.
   - governments can't control websites or email.
   - newspapers/TV companies can be sued if they get something badly wrong.

GLOSSARY

Freedom fighter: Someone who is prepared to use force to fight for freedom.

Political bias: Favouring one side more than another in news coverage.

Satellite television: Television via a satellite dish from a commercial company, i.e. Sky TV.

Terrestrial television: Television from a UK-land based organisation, i.e. BBC, ITV, Channels 4 and 5. Can be digital.

Terrorist: Someone who uses terror against civilians (ordinary people, not soldiers) to try to make the state give in/collapse – e.g. car bombings, parcel bombs.

Local Protest

This Green and Pleasant Land?

A 'NIMBY' is someone who does not want any changes in their local area.

They may not be against change, but they think it should happen somewhere else. NIMBY means 'Not In My Back Yard'.

People often object to new planning proposals. What would you say if your local council said your area was the best place to put one of the following?

- new airport runway
- new low cost housing
- waste incinerator
- a new road
- a centre for asylum seekers.

Would you be a NIMBY too? The nicer the place, the more locals want to keep it that way. They will often fight against proposals like this. But are they being fair? If everyone fights change it can end up dumped on the doorstep of those too weak to fight it. Some areas may miss out on useful development.

Local councils must plan for new housing and industry. Even if local councils don't want any change, they can be told to produce a Development Plan if the government has decided that new development is needed.

Devon County Council was told by the government that Devon needed to build 99,000 new homes between 1991 and 2011.

The council had to decide whether to add them to existing towns and villages, or whether to build new towns.

Devon decided to build **new towns**. One was to be in South Hams. Locals set up a **pressure group**, SHARD (South Hams Against Rural Destruction).

What Elements Make Up a Successful Campaign?

SHARD used different ways to campaign. It:

- recruited lots of members (to raise money and ideas);

▼ Rural South Hams.

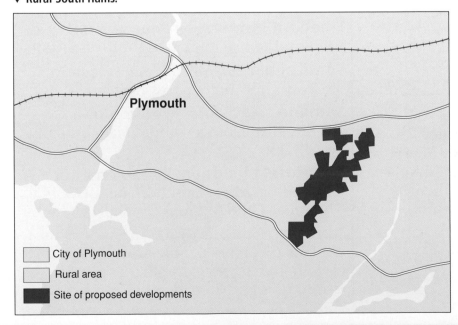

City of Plymouth

Rural area

Site of proposed developments

▼ SHARD protest.

- researched the issue so as to challenge the experts;
- used the media well. To make the public aware the group put out press releases, spoke on local radio and appeared on regional television. The group held numerous marches and protests to gain publicity.

Follow the progress of a local pressure group/campaign group in your area. How many of the elements of a successful campaign does it show?

? Questions

1 What do you think are acceptable arguments for change or against change? Where would you draw the line?
   - It would destroy rare plants, animals or birds.
   - It's the only green space left round here.
   - It will increase noise, air or water pollution.
   - It will bring the wrong sort of person to the area.
   - This area's very nice and it will spoil it.
   - This area's already got enough problems without this.
   - We need the jobs it will bring.
   - It's got to go somewhere.
   - without this the area will go downhill.
   - It'll bring money into the local economy.
   - We need new people and ideas round here. This will help.
   - It will make life more convenient.
2 What are the elements of a successful campaign?
3 Why is media coverage important to any local pressure group?

GLOSSARY

New towns: A entire new development, normally built on a greenfield site.

Pressure group: A group of people who share a common aim and work together to bring about change or prevent change. Pressure groups operate at all levels of society: local, regional, national and international.

Pressure for Change

KEY ISSUES

○ How do national pressure groups bring about change?

National Protest

Many more people belong to pressure groups than to political parties. The Royal Society for the Protection of Birds (RSPB) has more members than the three major UK political parties put together.

Pressure Groups

There are many different kinds of pressure groups.

1 Voluntary groups/non-profit-making groups or charities such as the RSPB. Groups like these were set up by people to promote their hobby or support a needy cause. But the RSPB also acts as a pressure group by campaigning to save habitats and rare birds.

2 Interest groups such as trade unions or the British Medical Association that protect the interests of their members.

3 Single-issue groups exist to campaign about one cause only. They can be set up by anyone. Successful ones attract media coverage and persuade the government to change policy.

i INFO BOX

The Snowdrop Campaign was set up to press parliament to tighten up handgun use after the Dunblane killings, when a teacher and many of her class were killed by a gunman. A national petition was successful in getting a majority of MPs to change the law.

Greenpeace is an international environmental group. It uses **non-violent direct action** (e.g. getting in the way of whaling ships by sailing its boats amongst them). It films its actions for the media. It also does independent scientific research, and actively lobbies governments and international organisations to bring about change.

The Downfall of a Prime Minister

In the late 1980s, many people became angry about the new Community Charge (Poll Tax) that was introduced by the Conservative government. Groups organised protest marches. Some people took **violent direct action**. MPs' post bags were full of complaints about the new tax. However, the Prime Minister, Mrs Thatcher, refused to ditch it. Public opinion turned against the Conservatives. They lost a parliamentary by-election. Conservatives thought they would have to change their policy or they would lose the next General Election. Mrs Thatcher resigned and Conservative MPs supported John Major in the leadership election. He became Prime Minister and brought in the Council Tax to replace the Poll Tax (see page 50).

Within the Law or Direct Action?

The Royal Society for the Prevention of Cruelty to Animals (RSPCA) campaigns within the law on issues such as hunting with hounds, factory farms and animal experimentation.

Governments consult the RSPCA about these issues.
But in the late 1990s people set up **non-violent direct action** groups to protest against the export of live animals from UK ports. People of all ages and backgrounds took part, many protesting in this way for the first time. Protesters blockaded docks, sitting down in front of lorries. Docks ground to a halt so the shipping companies refused to accept lorries carrying animals. The protesters had got what they wanted.

A Protest too Far?

Some forms of direct action are illegal, threatening or violent.

▲ May Day rioters attack MacDonalds, London 2000.

In 1998, 6,000 mink were set free from a fur farm by animal liberation activists. The group said this was justified because animal cruelty was as important an issue as banning slavery and women getting the vote. But escaped mink do a lot of damage, killing pets, farm animals and wild animals.

Global Protest

Groups like Greenpeace, Amnesty and Oxfam have always campaigned for global change using non-violent methods

But new direct action groups have sprung up, helped by the new media. The internet, e-mail and phone texting provide quick and cheap ways for people to pass on information and to organize themselves.

Some anti-capitalist protesters use violence to disrupt meetings of world leaders. International meetings are now often held in isolated, secure locations to prevent trouble.

GLOSSARY

Non-Violent direct action: Peaceful action to promote a cause.

a) Can be legal e.g. marches and lobbying.

b) May be illegal e.g. refusal to pay tax, obstructing a lorry. But these protesters break the law openly and accept the results.

Violent direct action: Violence against people or property to promote a cause e.g. breaking windows, rioting, breaking fences or equipment, throwing stones, threatening people because of their work. Usually these protesters try to avoid arrest.

❓ Questions

1 Choose the statement below that best fits your opinion about pressure group methods. Use examples from different times/places to prepare a speech which supports your view.
   - *'It is always wrong to break the law, however strongly you feel.'*
   - *'Non-violent direct action is justified if the cause is right. Protesters should be prepared to be arrested if they do something illegal.'*
   - *'Violent direct action is justified if the cause is right.'*

2 How does your view change if you are thinking about campaigning for change in a state that is not a democracy, where people could be arrested or tortured if they protest?

Our Role in the Wider World

▲ 10 new countries join the European Union in 2004.

The European Ideal

The European Union (then the EEC – European Economic Community) was set up in 1957 by politicians from 6 countries. Italy, Belgium, Holland and Luxembourg joined and all 6 signed the Treaty of Rome. France and Germany were founder members. They had often fought each other. But now they hoped to prevent another European war by bringing Europe together.

The European Union had *political aims*:

- to keep the peace and support democracy;
- to cooperate politically;
- to create its own power bloc which could compete against the superpowers of USA and Russia. (Russia was a communist system that controlled Eastern Europe. The USA was a capitalist system that supported democracy in Europe.)

The European Union also had *economic aims*:

- to expand trade and wealth;
- to create a common market for goods (free trade within the EU);
- to encourage regional development, especially in poorer areas.

The UK tried to join later. Its first applications for membership were turned down by the French. They said we 'weren't European enough, more concerned with our relationship across the Atlantic', meaning the USA who has traditionally been our close ally.

The UK became a member in 1973 and the first national referendum on our membership was held in 1975. A 2:1 majority voted to stay in.

By 1995 the EU had 15 members. In 2004 there will be 25, as 10 more from Eastern Europe join. (For more information on the EU see page 45).

Who Gets What?

Over a third of the EU budget goes to regional development. Poorer regions of the EU benefit from this, including Cornwall and Wales.

44.5 per cent of the EU budget is spent on financial support for farmers – the Common Agricultural Policy (CAP). Only 5 per cent of the EU workforce are farmers but they receive most EU money. There is an urgent need to reform CAP, especially as new entrants such as Poland have many poor farmers.

Why Do People Get So Angry About The EU?

- Sovereignty. Some people believe the EU, based in Brussels, is taking away sovereignty – the power of our national government to decide things in the UK.
- Common taxation system. Some countries want us to have the same levels of income

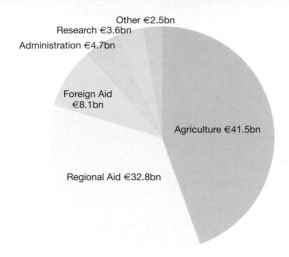

Other €2.5bn
Research €3.6bn
Administration €4.7bn
Foreign Aid €8.1bn
Agriculture €41.5bn
Regional Aid €32.8bn

tax and VAT across Europe. This would make a fairer trading market, but leave less power for each country to look after their own economies.

- The Euro (single European currency) means that individual countries have less independence over what they can spend or borrow as a country.

- Size. Some people believe EU decision-makers are out of touch with the feelings of ordinary people. This leads to low turnout in European elections.

- Democracy. Some say the EU is undemocratic, that it is controlled by the Council of Ministers, not by the Members of European Parliament (MEPs).

The other side of the coin
- Pooled sovereignty. By joining an international organisation you give some power away but you gain more because you have a say as part of a powerful organisation.

- Taxation. With a looser structure there is no need for common taxation. The EU is cheap – about the same as a quarter of our average Council Tax for each citizen.

- The single market already makes every EU country richer. The Euro would bring costs down even more. If the Euro was

used by all countries in the EU it would become a powerful world currency like the dollar.

- The EU is getting a new constitution to iron out problems. It has already been a remarkable success and gives us all opportunities to work, travel and participate as free European citizens.

- Democracy. MEPs are directly elected. Each country sends its ministers to make decisions in the Council of Ministers.

GLOSSARY

Federalism: The USA and Germany are federal. A constitution sets out how power is shared between federal and state governments. Each US State has its own laws and Governor. But the Federal Government has power over foreign policy and national issues.

? **Questions**

1. Why do so many people oppose the idea of a United States of Europe?
2. What are the advantages and the disadvantages of the UK belonging to the EU?

A New World Order

Two World Wars last century started in Europe. Tens of millions died. By the end of the Second World War in 1945 two super-powers dominated the world stage, the USA and the USSR (now known as Russia and the former Soviet States).

On 24 October 1945, after the end of the Second World War, the United Nations was set up in New York. The UN had two main aims:

1 The UN was planned to be an organisation where all the countries of the world could sort out their differences without violence. If need be, the UN could raise armed forces from its member countries to fight aggression or keep the peace.

2 The UN was expected to set up specialist agencies that would lead to the economic and social advancement of all.

UN Structure

There are two bodies which discuss and decide.

The General Assembly

Every single member country, however small, sends one representative. They meet annually to debate. The Assembly is a world forum. Resolutions made by the Assembly are not binding on members. However, a unanimous resolution is a very powerful comment.

The Security Council

Deals with conflict. It has five permanent members – USA, Russia, China, France and the UK. These five members have the power to 'veto' any decision of the Council.

Ten others are elected every two years by the Assembly.

So to get a 'resolution' through there has to be a majority vote that is not vetoed. Sometimes countries abstain.

The Security Council has the power to:

• Send in armies to fight directly to resolve conflicts (e.g. the Korean War).

• Send in peacekeeping troops to act as a buffer between armies of opposing countries or to stop civil war (such as between the Greek and Turkish forces in Cyprus). These forces often come from countries that are neutral, for example the Republic of Ireland.

• Send in weapons inspectors to enforce its resolutions (e.g. in Iraq in the 1990s)

Specialist Agencies – some examples

The UN Food Programme organises famine relief.

The United Nations High Commission for Refugees (UNHCR) provides help for 22 million refugees.

UNAIDS helps 33 million people suffering from the HIV virus.

UNRWA has provided schooling, health care and relief assistance to 3 million Palestinian refugees since 1950.

The UN Under Fire

Since the 1980s the UN has sometimes been criticised, especially by the USA. Critics say:

• the UN is slow and bureaucratic (tied by rules)

▲ The UN Food Programme gives food to starving people.

- it is just a talking shop
- it has no 'teeth'.

These countries have withdrawn financial contributions and favoured non-UN bodies such as the **World Bank**, the **WTO** and the **IMF**. These can be dominated by US interests. The UN budget is less than the New York Fire and Police Service combined and is currently owed 2.5 billion dollars by its member states. Over half of this money is owed by the USA.

▲ Blue Helmets UN Forces in action.

▲ UN HQ in New York.

ℹ INFO BOX

THE UN'S ACHIEVEMENTS

1 Maintaining peace and security. Has deployed over 40 peacekeeping forces.

2 Negotiating 172 peaceful settlements of disputes.

3 Promoting Democracy. Helped set up free and fair elections in 45 countries.

4 UN Development Programme (UNDP) supports 5000 projects.

5 Promoting Human Rights, Universal Declaration of Human Rights 1948.

6 Protecting the environment e.g. Earth Summit at Rio de Janeiro in 1992.

7 Preventing spread of nuclear weapons. UN staff inspect nuclear reactors in 90 countries.

8 Promoting independence in many countries that are now member states e.g. former colonial countries such as Sierra Leone.

9 Strengthening international law. It has aided over 300 agreements and treaties.

10 Handing down judicial decisions through the work of the International Court of Justice.

GLOSSARY

IMF: International Monetary Fund (see pages 98–101).

World Bank: Lends money to countries for development projects (see pages 98–101).

WTO: World Trade Organisation. Makes rules to enforce free trade between countries.

❓ Questions

1 In what ways has the UN helped preserve the peace since 1945?

2 Has the UN made a difference? If so, why are many of the world's population hungry and poor?

3 What powers do you think the UN should have over national governments?

The Extended British Family?

KEY ISSUES

○ What is the importance of the Commonwealth?

The Commonwealth

The Commonwealth is a unique 'family' of 54 nations. Some like Britain, Australia and Canada are **developed**. Others like Mozambique and Fiji are **developing** countries. Its people (1.7 billion) make up 30 per cent of the world's population. States from all over the world, of many races and cultures, come together as members. Every four years the Commonwealth Games are held. In 2002 these were in Manchester.

Britain's role

All members except one – Mozambique – used to be British colonies. But now Britain is just an ordinary member. The Commonwealth is a voluntary association of independent states. Its headquarters is the Commonwealth Secretariat in London, but its meetings are held throughout the world. Over 50 per cent of Britain's direct foreign aid goes to Commonwealth countries. (see pages 98–99)

The Queen is Head of State in Britain and also 15 other member countries.

Aims of the Commonwealth are:
to advance democracy, human rights and sustainable economic and social development in its member countries.

How? The Commonwealth has no constitution or charter, but the heads of government of the member states meet every two years to discuss issues of common interest. It cannot force the governments of member states to change their policies. But it can use its influence to investigate and criticise. It can suspend members so they miss out on the benefits of membership.

Examples:

- In 1993 it suspended Nigeria after its military regime sentenced to death writers who criticised the government.
- In 2000 it suspended Fiji when the elected government was overthrown.
- In 2002 it suspended Zimbabwe after Commonwealth observers said the country's presidential elections were unfair.

Membership also brings practical benefits through the Commonwealth Fund for Technical Co-operation (CFTC) which helps tackle poverty.

A Black and White Issue – Bringing South Africa in from the Cold

The Commonwealth tried for many years to campaign against apartheid in South Africa. But this was not easy. The white government left the Commonwealth in 1961.

South Africa had been a British colony between 1912 and 1948. Non-whites made up the vast majority of the population. The majority of the smaller white population were Afrikaners. They were of Dutch origin and wanted strict racial segregation – 'Apartheid'. They believed non-whites were inferior and must be kept separate. In 1948 The Afrikaner National Party won the General Election and introduced the apartheid system. This meant:

- Everyone was classified by their race.
- People from different races were not allowed to marry.
- Each race could only live in certain areas.

In practice non-whites were kept poor. In 1960 non-white representation in the parliament of South Africa was banned. Only whites had political rights. Non-whites were not allowed in certain shops, schools, or areas. Even park benches were for whites or non-whites.

The Fight against Apartheid

It took many years to force change. Different methods included:

1   In 1952 the African National Congress (ANC) started a campaign of peaceful resistance to apartheid.

2   When the vote was taken away the ANC decided to use violent methods against property (e.g. oil wells) as well. In 1964 Nelson Mandela and other ANC leaders were sentenced to life imprisonment for encouraging such acts of 'terrorism' against the apartheid regime.

3   In 1976 over 575 people died in Soweto in clashes with police.

4   International 'persuasion'. The UK government still carried on trading and cultural links with South Africa. It argued these would be more likely to make South Africa listen to reason than cutting all contact.

5   International sanctions. Some countries boycotted the country by ceasing to trade with South Africa.

6   Direct Action. South Africans of all races came to live in England and helped lead the protests. The Anti-Apartheid movement called on people to boycott (not buy) South African goods and to 'disinvest' in firms such as Barclays who had strong trading links. They demonstrated against white-only sports teams visiting the UK.

7   Neighbours. South Africa became more isolated when Zimbabwe, Mozambique and Namibia came to be governed by their black African majority.

The End of Apartheid

A new white President, De Klerk, realised that time had run out. He started negotiations with the leaders representing all groups in South Africa to bring about a peaceful transfer to majority rule. In 1990 Nelson Mandela and others were released from prison after 26 years.

▲ Nelson Mandela celebrates victory.

De Klerk and Nelson Mandela received the Nobel Peace Prize in 1993.

In 1994 the first non-racial elections were held and the ANC won. On 10 May 1994 Nelson Mandela was sworn in as President of South Africa and formed a government of National Unity. This included the African majority and white minority parties.

South Africa rejoined the Commonwealth in 1994, after an absence of 33 years.

GLOSSARY

Colony: A country ruled by another country.

Developed/developing: Describes the economies of richer and poorer countries.

? Questions

1   What should the Commonwealth/others do when it disapproves of what another country is doing?
2   Was the ANC right to use violent methods in the early 1960s?

International Conflict and Cooperation

KEY ISSUES

○ How do we get involved in disputes?
○ How can we resolve conflicts?

ℹ️ INFO BOX

TRUANCY MOTHER JAILED

The government is cracking down on truancy. Magistrates' Courts can now impose fines up to £2,500. As a last resort they can jail parents.

In May 2002 Patricia Amos was sentenced to prison because she did not make sure that two of her daughters attended their secondary school. The Court heard that the Local Education Authority had tried many ways to help. She had failed to attend meetings and had already broken a **parenting order** requiring her to make the girls attend school.

She appealed. Her sentence was reduced to 28 days. Her children now attend school. Mrs Amos says she has learned her lesson.

Consider who had rights, responsibilities and power in this case.

* Parent
* Government
* School
* Local Education Authority
* Children
* Courts

⏸️ Was this a successful way to resolve this dispute?

Why Do Conflicts Occur?

1 Sharing
Having to share often causes conflict. Sometimes it is sorted out by agreement. Sometimes the law is used. Sometimes conflict escalates (gets worse) and turns into fighting and full-scale war. People fight about:

* two tribes/religions/races sharing the same country (see pages 90–93).
* how to share property between friends and family when someone dies.
* surviving when there is not enough to go round.

2 Leaders
Usually more than one person wants to be leader. To avoid conflict groups develop rules for selecting leaders.

3 How much power should leaders have?
Today we try to control this conflict through political debate and elections.

4 Is it fair?
If some people think they are treated unfairly they may set up pressure groups, wage campaigns or take direct action.

5 Domination
Some groups seek to dominate other groups. This is a major source of conflict. Many civil and international wars have occurred over the years for this reason.

Is Conflict Always a Bad Thing?
Conflict can be useful.

* It makes us think more clearly if we have to put our case against others.
* It brings issues into the open and lets us deal with it. Dictatorships have more trouble dealing with conflict because there is no free speech. Opposition is often violent.
* Democracy is a major step forward in managing conflict. Disagreements can be expressed, discussed and voted on. People don't have to fight.

What Happens in Conflicts?
Most disputes go through stages.

- **First stage**: Each side wants something. A believes (s)he can only be satisfied if B loses. B believes (s)he can only be satisfied if A loses.
- **Second stage**: Escalation. Neither side actively seeks to resolve the dispute. The longer it goes on, the harder it becomes to sort it out. Conflict gets worse.
- **Third stage:** Attack. One side might be stronger than the other. It tries to win by imposing its solution so that the other side loses. This does not resolve the conflict. It may work in the short term. However in the long term the conflict goes on.

How disputes escalate (get worse)

Resentment. If one side feels it is being treated unfairly then it is determined not to 'give in'. It could retaliate – fight back. People could be hurt and property damaged. Bitterness grows.

Loss of face. Neither side wants to appear as the loser. This is a real obstacle when attempting to bring sides together, especially if many people have been affected by the conflict.

Conflict Resolution – How Conflicts are Resolved

It depends! Some conflicts cannot be resolved by **compromise**. If one side is completely unreasonable (e.g. discriminates or persecutes the other) then the other side must resist. At the same time it can try patient education and reasoning.

Conflict resolution means each side must recognise that the only way forward is to compromise.

Many conflicts may be resolved like this. If both parties are prepared to negotiate the following may help:

- Intermediaries. When parties do not trust each other, other people can be used to get messages across without face-to-face meetings.

- An arbitrator. Someone trusted by both sides who will hear the arguments and come up with a compromise proposal that both sides agree to accept.

▲ How could this dispute be resolved?

Two brothers aged 11 and 13 want to go out skateboarding until 10.30 p.m.

Their parents say they must do their homework first, and 10.30 p.m. is far too late. The boys think their parents are being unfair.

GLOSSARY

Compromise: For the sake of peace both sides give way on some of their demands.

Parenting order: The Court can make an order telling someone they must be a better parent, e.g. make their child go to school, attend parenting classes, enforce discipline etc.

 Questions

Look at the picture above.

1 How could this conflict escalate?
2 How could this conflict be resolved?

The UK and Conflict

In recent years the United Kingdom has been involved in several disputes with other nations. The UK has tried to resolve these in different ways.

Case 1: Falklands War

In April 1982 the Argentinians invaded the Falkland Islands in the South Atlantic. For over 100 years Argentina claimed these islands, which they call the Malvinas. The Falkland Islanders have always said they wish to remain British citizens and that the islands should remain British.

In 1982 Argentina was ruled by a military junta (dictatorship). The British had only a few soldiers on the Falklands. Argentina invaded with thousands of troops. The UK asked for United Nations support in condemning the invasion. The Falkland Islands are over 7,000 miles from the UK. The UK decided to retake the Falkland Islands. Three nuclear submarines guarded the area until the task force of 65 British ships and 15,000 men arrived.

▲ British troops arriving in the Falkland Islands during the Falklands War.

During the fight to retake the Islands, the British Navy destroyed over half of the Argentinian combat aircraft. The Argentinian cruiser Belgrano was torpedoed by a British submarine. The British Navy lost several ships to bombs and Exocet missiles.

The conflict ended on 14 June 1982 after a three-week campaign. The Argentines surrendered and the military junta lost power in Argentina.

The British lost 238 men.

How has peace been kept/the dispute resolved?

• The UK now keeps many more troops on the Falklands.

• UK and Argentina have agreed terms for oil and gas exploration in the South Atlantic.

• The Falkland Islands has an increasing population. More tourists visit. Development is funded by money raised from its sale of fishing rights.

• In 1998 the Argentinian President visited the UK.

Case 2: Hong Kong

In 1842 the British took over Hong Kong Island and in 1898 **leased** other land called the New Territories for 99 years.

Hong Kong is a big economic centre and one of the world's largest exporters. Communist China wanted it back. In 1984 the UK government agreed to hand back both the New Territories and Hong Kong in 1997.

Why did it do this? It knew Hong Kong could not survive on its own. Britain could not defend Hong Kong against a huge power like China. The peaceful handover allowed the British government to negotiate the following conditions for the future:

• The 'life style' of Hong Kong would remain unchanged for 50 years.

• a high degree of self government with no communist system imposed upon it.

▲ Hong Kong and mainland China.

▲ Gibraltar in relation to Spain.

Case 3: Gibraltar – 'Between a Rock and a Hard Place'?

Gibraltar was given to Britain in the Treaty of Utrecht (1713). Gibraltar is a tiny 6.5 sq km outcrop from Spain, with a population of 30,000. Gibraltar was the British Navy's way to control the Mediterranean. It is still an important military base.

For many years Spain has claimed **sovereignty** over Gibraltar. From 1969 to 1985 it closed its frontier gates to Gibraltar. Recently the British government started talks with the Spanish government about the future of Gibraltar. Spain and the United Kingdom are members of the EU and get on well as partners. Many British citizens retire to Spain. Both sides would like to sort out this long-standing issue. But the people of Gibraltar want to stay British. In 1967, 12,138 voted for no change in their status and 44 against.

'They should negotiate even though the people of Gibraltar don't want them to.'

Do you agree?

GLOSSARY

Lease: A legal agreement to control land for a certain number of years in return for money.

Sovereignty: The right of a country to govern itself.

? Questions

1 What international conflicts involving Britain are in the news at the moment?
2 Match these conflicts to the ways they were resolved.

Falklands   **War** – direct use of the British armed forces.
Hong Kong   **Military Action** – use of British troops/navy/RAF as part of international
Gibraltar   action by NATO/EU/UN.
Kosovo   **Direct Negotiation** – Britain dealt face to face to make an agreement.
Iraq   **Arbitration** – Britain relied on a third party (an independent agency such as the UN) to help come up with solutions.
   Still to be resolved – the dispute carries on.

3 Discuss your views on these issues:
   – How and why the UK reacted differently to the problem of Hong Kong and the Falkland Islands.
   – When is military force justified?

People Who Have Made a Difference

Mohandas (Mahatma) Gandhi	Famous worldwide for making a difference
Martin Luther King	" "
Nelson Mandela	" "
John Hume	Won 1998 Nobel Peace Prize for their contribution to
David Trimble	conflict resolution in Northern Ireland

Mahatma Gandhi

Gandhi was born in India in 1869. He came to London and trained as a lawyer. He moved to South Africa and worked hard to improve the rights of Indian workers. Here he developed his ideas of passive resistance – the use of non-violent action against injustice. He was often jailed.

From 1915 he led the campaign for Indian independence from the British. Tax boycotts, sit-down strikes and huge demonstrations were used. But if Muslim or Hindu supporters used violence, he would fast until the violence ended. In 1947 the British granted India independence, but fighting broke out between Hindus and Muslims and the country was partitioned into India and Pakistan. Gandhi fasted to stop the rioting. He was assassinated in January 1948, when he was about to take evening prayers. His killer was an Indian who opposed Gandhi's religious tolerance.

Martin Luther King

Martin Luther King was a black American who led the struggle for racial equality that ended segregation in the USA.

Even though the US Supreme Court ruled against segregation in 1954, many aspects of life, especially in the southern states of the USA, continued along segregated lines. Rosa Parks, a black woman, was thrown off a bus and fined for refusing to give up her seat to a white man. Six-year-old Ruby Bridges was spat on for wanting to go to the same school as white children.

Martin Luther King used the power base of the black church to campaign for change. He founded an organisation calling for a non-violent struggle against racism, leading marches and boycotts to bring about change. His life was often threatened. He was hounded by the FBI, who bugged his phone. In 1964 he won the Nobel Peace Prize.

He was assassinated in 1968 in Memphis. Since 1983 his birthday has been a national holiday in the USA.

Nelson Mandela – from Prisoner to President

Nelson Mandela was born in South Africa in 1918. He trained as a lawyer and became leader of the ANC which organised peaceful resistance to apartheid (pages 82–83). When all political rights were taken from non-whites the ANC started training members to use armed resistance as well.

In 1962 he was jailed for life by the Government. But he still believed in a free and multi-racial South Africa. He was prepared, when the time came, to talk to and work alongside the people who had kept him

▲ Nelson Mandela.

▲ Mohandas Gandhi.

in jail. He was released in 1990. He prepared South Africa for the handover to black majority rule. He was elected first president of the new South African government in 1994. His message was reconciliation (peace and friendship) with the whites, not revenge for the years of injustice. This helped the peaceful changeover. He shared the Nobel Peace Prize with FW de Klerk in 1993.

Northern Ireland

Ireland was partitioned in 1922. Northern Ireland had a majority of Protestants. These were Unionists who wanted to remain in the United Kingdom. The rest of Ireland (Eire) became independent. Ireland has a majority of Catholics.

Nationalists (Catholics) in Northern Ireland still wanted a united Ireland.

They complained they were denied their civil rights by the Unionists. In 1968 there were riots and people were driven out of their houses because of their religion. The British army sent in troops to keep the peace.

Some **republicans** joined **paramilitary** groups such as the IRA and used terrorism against the British and the **loyalists**. Some loyalists set up their own terrorist groups. For nearly thirty years there were outrages in Northern Ireland, Ireland and the UK. These included car, shopping centre and pub bombings in Belfast, Birmingham, Canary Wharf and Manchester. In 1984 the IRA blew up the Imperial Hotel Brighton in an attempt to kill Prime Minister Margaret Thatcher and all her ministers. 'Tit for tat killings' continued in Northern Ireland.

The British and Irish governments both wanted a peaceful political solution to the 'Troubles'. But they had to find a way which involved both sides of the divided community in a settlement. Eventually this would have to involve talking to the former paramilitaries. The aim was to get all sides to give up violence and use ordinary politics to argue their case.

(i) INFO BOX

THE GOOD FRIDAY AGREEMENT

1993: The Anglo-Irish Declaration laid out a framework for achieving agreement. There must be 'consent' – any settlement could only go ahead if agreed by the people of Northern Ireland.

1996: George Mitchell (a former US senator) agreed to chair the peace talks.

1996–8: Leader of the Unionist Party David Trimble and leader of the nationalist Social Democratic and Labour Party (SDLP) John Hume put aside years of mistrust to help bring the two sides together in talks involving all parties.

Good Friday 1998: The Agreement was announced. A new Assembly was created in Northern Ireland to run most things locally. Referendums in Northern Ireland and Ireland supported this. David Trimble became First Minister in a coalition government including all parties. Sinn Fein (republicans such as Martin McGuiness) were involved too.

GLOSSARY

Loyalists: Northern Irish Protestants who are loyal to the Queen and British rule.

Paramilitaries: People who organise themselves like an army and use violence, murder and terrorism.

Republicans: Irish nationalists (Catholics) who want the whole of Ireland completely independent from Britain.

(?) Questions

1 Find out what has happened since to the Peace Process.
2 What are the chances for long-term peace in Northern Ireland?

A Bitter Conflict

This has been one of the bitterest conflicts of the twentieth and twenty-first centuries.

How did the conflict start? Can a lasting settlement be finally achieved? Before you can discuss this you need to understand the background. The conflict started when two groups of people wanted to live in the same land.

History until 1947

Look at the map. The land that is now called Israel used to be called Palestine before 1947. The Jews came originally from there – it was their 'promised land'. Jerusalem is their holy city. But many centuries ago most left and settled all over Europe and North Africa. The majority of the population of Palestine has been Arab since then. Most Palestinians are Muslim. Some are Christian. Jerusalem is a holy city to both Muslims and Christians.

Zionism

In the early twentieth century some Jews began to press for their own 'homeland' where they would not be persecuted. They believed Palestine had been promised by God to the Jews. So these 'Zionists' decided to return to Palestine and try to set up their homeland there. This return was unpopular with the Palestinians. They felt threatened by the idea of large-scale Jewish immigration and the idea of their land being taken over.

The British governed Palestine after the First World War. They allowed some Jewish immigration and tried to keep the peace between Arabs and Jews.

During the Second World War millions of European Jews were murdered by the Nazis. There was new pressure after the war for a homeland where Jews could set up their own state and be safe. The Arabs in Palestine didn't see why it had to be on their land. By 1947 Jews were 36% of the population. In 1914 they had been 8%.

Jewish terrorist groups such as Irgun committed atrocities against the British and Arab civilians.

The Creation of Israel/The Palestinians Leave

In 1947 the US Government decided to back the creation of a Jewish State in Palestine. They strongly supported the UN proposal to partition (split) Palestine into a Jewish State and an Arab State.

The Palestinians and the Arab States rejected this. But the State of Israel was declared on 14 May 1947. The Arab States attacked the Israeli army. The Israelis won and drove most of the Palestinians from their homes. 400,000 Palestinians settled in refugee camps in various Arab lands, but mostly in the West Bank area of the River Jordan, which was now controlled by Jordan.

This war is celebrated as the War of Independence by the Israelis. It is called the 'Catastrophe' by the Palestinians.

This shows the huge differences that remain between the two sides. Both sides think they are right and the other side is wrong.

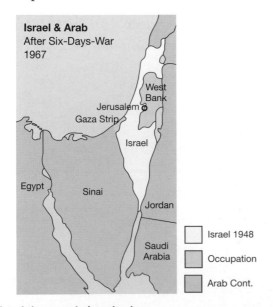

Israel & Arab
After Six-Days-War
1967

West Bank
Jerusalem
Gaza Strip
Israel
Egypt
Sinai
Jordan
Saudi Arabia

☐ Israel 1948
☐ Occupation
☐ Arab Cont.

▲ Israel and the occupied territories.

Since 1947 – The Israeli Version of Events

'A new modern democratic state was set up where finally we Jews got to control our own fate. There has been great progress here. Enterprises such as irrigating the desert to grow oranges have improved the land. New modern cities thrive. All Jews have the right to come here to be safe from persecution.

But Israel has been under constant threat since then. The surrounding Arab states have never accepted Israel's right to exist.

In 1967 the Arab states attacked us from all sides. In this Six Day War the Israeli army succeeded in beating the Arabs and occupying the West Bank, the Gaza Strip and the whole of Jerusalem. Israel has never given this territory back because it is essential to our security. Since 1964 when the PLO (Palestinian Liberation Organisation) was set up Israel has been threatened by Arab terrorists. These people want to drive the Israelis into the sea. Many Israelis think we should permanently extend our borders to include the occupied territories. This is the land of Greater Israel, which the bible says God promised to the Jews. That is why we have built new Jewish settlements in the Arab lands of East Jerusalem, and the West Bank. This is rightfully our land now. The Arabs can always go somewhere else.'

Now read the experiences of two young Israelis.

Ruth lives in a Jewish settlement on the West Bank.

'My school bus has a military escort because of the danger from gangs of Arabs. (She refuses to call them Palestinians). They threw a rock at our car window. It is impossible to prove who has the right to this land. Arabs should leave and go to another country.

My idea of peace is not having to be afraid of Arabs; not having to have an escort to school.'

Jacob lives near Jerusalem

'I am a member of Peace Now, a group which works for peace. I have met and talked to Palestinians and now understand them better. But people at school call me a traitor and say I am soft on Arabs. My parents' car has been vandalised by other Jews. I think the only way forward is if more Jews and Palestinians meet face to face and talk.'

▲ The Jewish settlement of Ofarim on the West Bank.

▲ Bethlehem on the West Bank. Israeli tanks block access.

? Questions

1 Why do Israelis mistrust the Palestinians?
2 Why have the Israelis built settlements on the West Bank?

The Palestinian Version of Events

'Israel was set up by force without the consent of the majority Palestinian population. Our people were driven from the homes and farms they had lived in for centuries. We have lived in wretched refugee camps ever since. The Israelis have always refused to allow us any compensation or the right to return. US aid and military help have made Israel rich. The Arab nations tried to help by sending their armies against Israel. But the Six Day War made things even worse because the Israelis illegally occupied East Jerusalem, the Gaza Strip and the West Bank. Israel has ignored all the UN resolutions calling on it to withdraw to the pre-1967 borders. They keep stealing Arab land to build new settlements, filling them with people who have only just come over from the West and taking the water from our wells. We have to fight back against this oppression. We must have a proper state of our own.'

Now read the experiences of two young Palestinians.

Maysoon lives in a Palestinian refugee camp on the West Bank.

'My family originally came from a village near Jerusalem. They had orchards, olive groves and vineyards. In 1948 the Israeli army took over the village and destroyed most of the houses. They even dug up the cemetery.

I remember the Israeli planes attacking our refugee camp. I can never forgive them. Jews will have to learn to share the land. It will take a long time for the bad feelings between Jews and Palestinians to heal. I long to be able to move about freely and feel safe.'

Monzir lives in Gaza. He was 8 when the **intifada** started.

'I joined other children throwing stones. The Israelis imposed curfews to try to keep control. We just had to sit at home all day. We couldn't go to school. We were only allowed out for half an hour each week to do shopping.

I believe in peace. The Koran calls for peace. But peace will only come if we have the right to education, to move freely, to have our own state and passports and our own national identity. Jerusalem must be our capital.'

▲ A Palestinian refugee camp.

Trying to Resolve the Conflict

Outside powers have been heavily involved in peace efforts. The United Nations, Arab nations and Israel itself have been involved in different initiatives. The USA has been heavily involved in getting the two sides to negotiate. The latest attempt is a 'road map' proposed by President Bush in 2003. But many obstacles remain.

- Extremists on both sides who do not want to negotiate but want to dominate, e.g. Israelis who won't accept the idea of a Palestinian State and Palestinians who won't accept the idea of an Israeli state.

- Racist stereotyping. Some on each side talk as if the others don't count and don't have human feelings or rights.

- Religious intolerance. Some on each side believe God is on their side.

- Interference by outsiders. The big powers e.g. USA are not trusted because they have taken sides in the past. Arab states have supported terrorist groups.

- Violence. Suicide bomber and terrorist attacks by Palestinian groups like **Hamas** damage chances to build trust. Violent reprisals against Palestinians by the Israeli army damage Palestinian leaders who want to negotiate. They mean people won't support leaders who are seen as too soft with the Israelis.

- Bitterness. Some find it too hard to forgive and forget. They don't believe the other side really wants peace.

So what would help? See pages 84–85 for ideas.

- Compromise. Both sides have to give up something to achieve a settlement both can accept as fair.

- Willingness to be realistic about what can be achieved.

- Outside pressure must be balanced. Arbitrators must be fair.

---

i INFO BOX

A DIFFICULT ROAD TO PEACE

1977 At the Camp David talks Egypt made peace with Israel. But the Egyptian president was then assassinated by Arab extremists.

1993 In Oslo all parties agreed a way forward to be finalised in 1998.

1995 the Israeli Prime Minister was shot dead by a Jewish extremist.

1998 Extremists on both sides derailed the peace process because they weren't prepared to compromise. Although a Palestinian Authority was set up to govern the West Bank and Gaza it was not a State and lacked resources.

2001 The Palestinians started their intifada once more – uprisings in the occupied territories. Terrorist groups have attacked civilians in Israel with suicide bombings. Israel has used its army to attack the Palestinian Authority and civilians with aircraft, missiles and tanks in an attempt to capture the extremists. Roadblocks and checkpoints have stopped Palestinians travelling to their work.

2003 A 'road map' to peace was proposed by President Bush. For the first time the USA committed itself to a viable Palestinian State.

GLOSSARY

HAMAS: One of the Palestinian groups, which uses armed resistance and terrorism against Israeli soldiers and civilians.

Intifada: Palestinian resistance and uprising against Israel's control of the occupied territories.

? Questions

1 Why do Palestinians want the Israeli settlements removed?
2 Find out what has happened since to the Peace Process.
3 What are the chances for long-term peace in this area?

Globalisation

KEY ISSUES
○ What is ethical trading?
○ What is 'Fair Trade'?

Going Shopping – Making Choices

When you go shopping what makes you buy one item rather than another? Do you ask about:

Name?   Price?   Brand?   Quality?

Or do you want to use your power as a consumer to make ethical choices? Do you ask:

Local or multinational company?

Environmentally friendly?

Good conditions for the employees?

Child labour involved?

Tested on animals?

Wasteful packaging?

Recyclable?

Uses genetically modified (GM) food?

Uses additives and preservatives?

If you are concerned about these questions you will want to know if the company has an ethical trading policy. Ethical trade looks after the interests of the producer, retailer and consumer equally. Often there are codes of conduct covering wages and conditions.

Case Study – The Greenline Trading Policy

Firms sign up who want to show they are Fair, Ethical and Organic.

All the products sold are:

• People friendly – they do not exploit people in their production. Many products are 'fair-traded' giving producers

a fair return and support for their communities in poor countries.

• Animal friendly – they do not involve cruelty.

• Environment friendly – they do not cause damage to the environment. All food products are organic. Producers try to operate without using paper. Where this is unavoidable only paper which is 100% recycled is used. Wherever possible goods are sent out in re-used packaging, which would otherwise be sent to landfill.

Good for Business?

Firms such as Body Shop grew rich on the basis of their ethical trading policies. Simple packaging and natural products not tested on animals appeal to a growing market in richer countries. Now many major stores are copying at least some of their methods.

ⓘ INFO BOX

• In the USA, 85% of large companies have ethical trading codes of practice.

• Marks and Spencer has an ethical trading policy; they visit their suppliers and seek assurance regarding child labour and working conditions.

• EU Demands Ethical Reports. In May 2002 the EU parliament voted to demand that multinational companies publish in their annual reports the social and environmental impact of their businesses.

• A recent poll across Europe showed that 20% of consumers boycott goods on ethical grounds.

Fair Trade

Some consumers want to be sure that more of their money is going directly to the small farmers who grow, produce or make goods in poor countries. Fair Trade companies guarantee producers receive the best possible price for their products. You can find Fair Trade coffee and chocolate in some supermarkets as well as charities like Oxfam.

> Do you support this idea?
>
> Are you prepared to pay more for their products?

◀ Fair Trade goods ensure a fair wage for the worker.

In the past few years there has been a rapid increase in demand for organic food – food produced without any fertilisers, pesticides or weedkillers.

🗣 *'I want to be sure I'm not being poisoned by chemicals.'*

🗣 *'I want to support the countryside, not big business.'*

Or

🗣 *'I want cheap food'.*

🗣 *'I want my fruit and veg looking nice, all the same size with no blemishes.'*

> Which person is likely to buy organic?
>
> Which person is likely to buy non-organic supermarket food?

Globalisation

However, globalisation and the role of multinationals is still a big issue.

* Companies make profits from processing and packaging the goods.

▲ Fair Trade Rally, June 2002, at the House of Commons.

* Supermarkets drive down the prices paid to farmers both in the UK and poor countries.
* More people in the West rely on ready made processed food.
* Goods are transported all around the world, not sold locally.

GLOSSARY

GM Food: Genetically Modified Food (see pages 108–9).

Landfill: Digging big holes in the ground to bury rubbish.

Organic: Crops grown/animals raised using no artificial chemicals or pesticides.

❓ Questions

1 How can you, as a consumer, apply pressure on companies to trade ethically?
2 Design a survey to investigate the opinions of students, teachers and parents on Ethical, Fair and Organic trade.
  Possible Survey Questions. (Tip: You may want to provide a range of answers for them to tick.)
  – What would cause you to boycott goods?
  – What information do you look at on the label?
  – Would you be more or less likely to buy something that is
    a) organic   b) Fairly traded?
  – Do you mind paying more for organic/ fair trade goods?

Globalisation

Who are the Multinationals?

A multinational corporation is a company that operates in more than one country. There are now 63,000 multinational corporations in the world, and between them they are responsible for two-thirds of global trade and 80% of investment. They are the economic force behind **globalisation**.

Why Do People Worry About Them?

- They get basic raw materials like wood, cotton, cocoa and sugar from LDCs (Less Developed Countries – where agriculture is the largest employer.). Do they pay producers a fair price? Do they damage the environment there? Does this keep the country tied to one crop and so keep it poor?

- They export and then process the goods in other countries such as Indonesia. Do they employ children? Do they pay fairly and provide safe conditions for their workers?

- They open and close factories all over the world, moving from one country to another where the wages are cheaper. How does it affect jobs and the whole community when they move?

▲ Child working conditions can be appalling.

- They exist to make a profit for shareholders, not for their workers or the countries they operate in. Do they pay their taxes or benefit the economy of these countries?

- Big multinationals have bigger incomes than the GNP (Gross National Product) of many smaller countries. Can they be controlled in an increasingly global economy?

ℹ INFO BOX

Low Pay

In Indonesia in July 2002 the entry level full-time wage in a factory making goods for a multinational company was about £1.40 per day.

Poor working conditions:

'You have to meet the quota before you can go home.'

'She hit all 15 team leaders in turn from the first one to the fifteenth…the physical pain didn't last long, but the pain I feel in my heart will never disappear.'

Two women workers in a LDC describing their conditions at work.

▲ A closed factory in Yorkshire.

 What do you think about this? Is price everything?

CADBURY SCHWEPPES – OUR POLICY

Cadbury Schweppes plc aims to act in a socially responsible manner at all times and asks it suppliers to adhere to policies which include:

- No forced labour.
- Employees can join trade unions.
- Children are employed only under circumstances that protect them from physical risks and do not disrupt their education.
- No harassment in the workplace.
- A healthy and safe work environment for each employee.
- Reasonable working hours and pay comparable to those offered by similar companies.

Cadbury Schweppes

Cadbury Schweppes is an example of a multinational aware of these concerns. It has introduced a Human Rights and Ethical Trading policies to make this clear to workers and customers.

 Does this policy reassure you? What questions would you still want answered?

Pressure Group Concerns About Multinationals

Many pressure groups are concerned about how a large number of multinational

▲ The Annual General Meeting (AGM) of a large multinational.

companies operate. Oxfam Community Aid Abroad demands that companies should ensure that:

- workers are allowed to join trade unions;
- international labour standards are respected;
- workers are paid a full-time wage which allows them to provide for themselves and their families;
- the demands they place on factory owners for low prices and fast production do not undermine workers' rights.

Companies should also cooperate with trade unions and credible human rights groups to verify that these policies are being implemented.

 Do you agree?

Who Controls the Multinationals?

Most multinationals are public companies (plc). They are accountable to their shareholders. Usually a majority of the shares are held by pension funds or banks on behalf of their investors. Individual shareholders often have very little control of these companies and are out-voted at meetings by the institutional shareholders (pension funds etc.)

GLOSSARY

Globalisation: Ability to produce goods anywhere in the world from materials from anywhere, and sell the product or service anywhere and keep profits in any country.

? Questions

1 What are the advantages and disadvantages to a LDC of multinational companies setting up factories in their country?
2 How could multinational companies be made more accountable?

Globalisation

KEY ISSUES

- Foreign aid – why give it?
- Foreign debt – keeping the poor poor?
- Can individuals make a difference?

Giving a Helping Hand

▲ Celebrities help to raise funds for people in need.

Charities often ask for money to help those abroad. Natural disasters like earthquakes, civil war or drought lead to starvation. Events such as Live Aid have raised many millions of pounds to help those in need. The UK government also gives millions in **foreign aid** each year.

The United Nations has set targets for donor countries of 0.7% – less than 1% of their **GNI**. Almost all the rich countries of the world have failed to reach this target.

Foreign Aid as a % of GNI in 2000	
United Kingdom	0.32%
France	0.32%
Germany	0.27%
Australia	0.27%
Denmark	1.06%
USA	0.10%

Which is the only country to have achieved more than the target?

Which country is most behind the target?

In 2001 the total aid given by rich countries to poor countries went down. In the UK the Chancellor of the Exchequer has promised that the UK will do more to help the poorest countries. The UK has already 'written off' some overseas debts owed to it.

The Weight of Debt

The poorest countries often suffer from natural disasters and civil war. In the past their governments borrowed heavily from individual governments or organisations such as the World Bank (see page 101). In Africa the interest payments alone are now more than four times their education or health budgets. In 1996 the OECD Development Assistance Committee agreed targets.

1 Reducing the proportion of people living in extreme poverty.
2 Progress towards universal primary education.
3 More girls in primary and secondary education.
4 Reducing maternal and under 5 mortality.
5 Increasing access to reproductive health services.
6 Reducing loss of environmental resources.

Case Study

Rwanda is one of the poorest countries in the world. 45% of the population live on less

▲ How can you refuse?

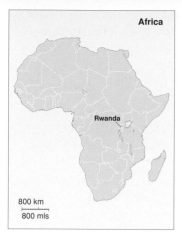

▲ Rwanda – one of the poorest countries in the world.

than 60p a day. The **GNP** is $180 US per head compared to the UK's $18,700 US. Rwanda owes $1 billion. It is already $100 million in arrears of interest payments.

A committee of British MPs has urged that Rwanda have its debts written off so that it can recover economically. What do you think?

The UN says that if debt were written off these countries could make improvements that in Africa alone would save the lives of 21 million children and provide 90 million girls and women with access to basic services.

ⓘ INFO BOX

American Foreign Aid. While US government aid might look very generous, two-thirds of it goes to just two countries: Israel and Egypt. (Much is spent on arms.) The remaining third is used to promote US exports or to fight the war against drugs. Some people argue this aid 'does not aid'. Because of the interest payments and the tied aid system, the US actually gets back more than it gives in foreign aid. Tied aid must be spent on goods from the donor country. The USA often uses this form of aid e.g. buying American grain to go to Ethiopia. Charities say it is better to give money than goods because then it goes to local farmers and develops the economy.

Why don't rich countries commit themselves to reach the target of 0.7%? This is a political problem.

- Other priorities come up. For example, the US recently increased its military budget by $100 billion dollars. Europe subsidises its agriculture to keep its farmers happy, but demands that poor nations open their markets to foreign competition.

- Political parties know there are votes in improving public services at home and keeping taxes down. But they are not confident voters would approve of more taxpayers' money being given to the poorest countries.

Can we, as individuals make a difference? Bond is a pressure group that suggests that we:

- Write to the Chancellor of the Exchequer.
- Write to the Prime Minister or our MP.

 Do you think this would help?

GLOSSARY

Foreign aid: Money or goods given by one government to another.

GNI: Gross National Income – the total yearly income of a country.

GNP: Gross National Product – the total amount of money earned by a country.

❓ Questions

1 Why do countries give foreign aid?
2 What rules would you draw up to allocate UK overseas aid?
3 How would debt relief help the rich countries as well as the poor countries?

Globalisation

What is the Biggest Threat to the World's Stability and Future?

Over-population? The birth rate in the poorer countries is much higher than in the rich countries

Or

Growing difference between rich and poor nations? People in developed countries own 87% of the world's vehicles, receive over 80% of the world's total income and have most of the world's food. Poor countries still owe billions of pounds worth of debt. It is becoming more difficult for the poor to make a living and grow enough food to survive.

Or

Environmental problems? People in developed countries make up 20% of the world's population. But they consume over 86% of the world's total resources. Climate change, floods and droughts will make things even worse for the people in poorer countries, even though they aren't responsible for most of the greenhouse gases.

Or are these all part of the same problem? – The rich get richer and the poor get poorer.

Many say the events of 11 September 2001, when terrorists flew planes into the World Trade Centre in America, partly reflect the frustration of the 'have-nots' against those who have so much.

This poverty and inequality leads to security problems for the rich countries as well.

- Civil wars create millions of refugees.
- Dictatorships mean people need asylum in the West.

- People-trafficking increases as desperate immigrants try to enter rich countries illegally.
- Drug-trafficking grows since poor farmers can make more money from growing drugs than growing food.
- Jealousy and resentment stirs hatred between different races.

 What could help?

Drop the Debt

Many believe that the time has come to write off the enormous debts. Jubilee Debt Campaign is a pressure group which campaigns for the cancellation of *all* the debts of the developing countries.

This UK-based group harassed the World Bank and the **IMF (International Monetary Fund)** for more than five years, asking them and the governments of the wealthy nations to give the poor countries a break.

Jubilee Debt Campaign says

🗣 *'It is morally right to help those who are so poor.'*

🗣 *'We owe the developing nations because of past exploitations. Britain and America grew rich*

▲ Jubilee Debt Campaign is supported by many celebrities, including Muhammad Ali, Quincy Jones and Bono (above).

by raiding Africa to take people as slaves. Europeans took 185,000 kilos of gold and 16 million kilos of silver from Latin America. Colonists and corporations seized land, labour, minerals and timber from many parts of the world, and never paid any compensation.'

Of the **G8** nations, Britain has led the way by writing off millions of pounds of debt owed by the poorest nations.

The World Bank

The World Bank is an associate of the United Nations. It lends money to its 183 member nations. This is spent on economic development.

The United States, Japan, Germany, France and the United Kingdom pay most to the World Bank, and so they have the most say about who gets what. However, all members are shareholders in the bank. The money comes from three main sources:

- Subscriptions paid by member countries.
- Selling bonds on the world's financial markets.
- Earnings from the bank's assets.

What Does the Bank Do?

'We share the same world, and we share the same challenge. The fight against poverty is the fight for peace, security, and growth for us all.' James D. Wolfensohn, President of the World Bank.

The bank lends money to help development in Africa, Asia, the Middle East and Latin America. In 2000, £12 billion was loaned.

▲ The World Bank lends money to improve housing and sanitation.

The bank says it is working towards a world that is free of poverty, and that it invests money in projects it believes will lead the developing countries towards economic stability such as clean water and sanitation. However, some criticise the Bank for supporting projects which don't really help the poorest farmers, and may do harm.

Example:
Hydroelectric dams which **displace** people.
Roads which carve through tropical forests.

GLOSSARY

Displace: Force people to leave their homes.

G8: The world's seven richest nations, plus Russia.

IMF – International Monetary Fund: This international organisation requires countries to pay back their debts and keep their currencies stable.

? Questions

1 Design a poster showing the dangers for the future if poor nations continue to get poorer.
2 List your ideas for helping the poorest countries.

▲ The World Bank president, James Wolfensohn.

Global Interdependence

Global Interdependence

KEY ISSUES

○ What are the problems of population growth?
○ What are the pressures on the environment?

It took until 1830 for the world's population to reach 1 billion. By 1930, it was 2 billion; by 1960, 3 billion; by 1975, 4 billion; by 1986, 5 billion and in 1999 it reached 6 billion.

The world's population is growing at a rate of nearly 80 million a year.

Why?

People are living longer.

More young people are surviving.

The growth is mainly in LDCs. Poorer people need more children to work on the land and help look after them when they are old. In richer countries the birth rate tends to go down, especially when women work and get a good education.

Is This a Problem?

It is a problem if people are too poor to feed their families.

They cut wood for cooking fuel → The forests decline.
The forests decline → The topsoil erodes.
The topsoil erodes → The deserts expand.
The deserts expand → The climate changes.

More and more people, desperate to survive, create shortages of water and food in many developing regions.

Desertification (expanding deserts) is a growing problem in Africa, Asia, Latin America, the Caribbean, and the northern Mediterranean. There is need for action on a global scale. If not, one-quarter of the Earth's surface could turn into desert. 12 million people already die each year because they have not got safe drinking water.

The United Nations has asked countries to sign up to a desertification convention. Every African country realises the threat and they are among the 169 countries that have signed so far. This convention commits countries to fighting desertification at national and regional levels. This will be done by passing laws to protect the environment.

Lake Chad

Lake Chad is getting smaller. It used to be one of the largest freshwater lakes in Africa. On one side are the rainforests. To the north is the Sahara Desert. Forty years ago the lake covered 25,000 square kilometres. Now it is one-twentieth of that size.

The annual monsoons used to fill the lake and water the crops. But since the late 1960s there have been terrible droughts. The Sahara Desert is advancing. People now have to take their irrigation water from the lake and the rivers to grow food.

Overgrazing by animals has led to a drier climate. The lack of grass and trees means that less moisture is now recycled back into the atmosphere. This has resulted in even less monsoon rain.

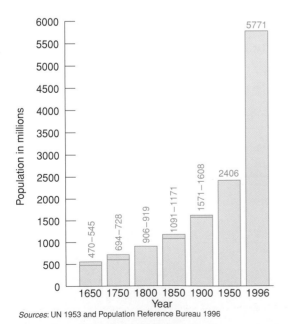

Sources: UN 1953 and Population Reference Bureau 1996

▲ Increase in population 1650–1996.

▼ This map of Africa shows Lake Chad and Tanzania.

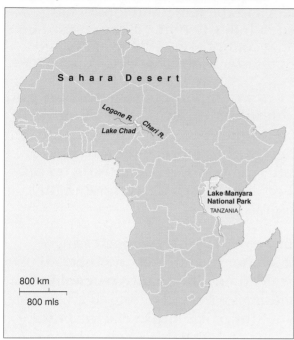

▼ The eland, oryx and kudu are no longer found in Tanzania's national park.

Tanzania

The same problems are happening in East Africa.

The land dries up → farmers cut down or burn trees to make new fields.
The new land is ploughed too deeply and soon the soil is exhausted → farmers cut down more trees to make new fields.

This is what has happened in Tanzania. Timber is the country's most important source of energy, giving over 90% of Tanzania's energy supply. Farmers also burn large areas of forest to clear land for crops. The result is vast environmental destruction and the drying up of some of the rivers. Many species of birds, animals and even trees are threatened.

It is reported that eland, oryx and kudu are no longer found in the Lake Manyara National Park. With more than 400,000 hectares of forests destroyed each year, it is estimated that half the country will be covered by sand within the next 50 years unless action is taken now.

What can be done? Tanzania's government is encouraging the planting of trees to try to slow down the march of the sands and to limit the environmental damage.

? Question

1 Development experts have suggested the following ideas for tackling these problems. Which do you think will work best and why?
 – Give girls at least a primary education.
 – Vaccinate babies to give parents confidence their children will survive.
 – Protect forest, savannah and wildlife reserves.
 – Educate farmers in farming methods that retain the soil's goodness.
 – Educate people in safe birth control techniques.
 – Ban the burning of forests.

This planet is our only home; it is the only place we know of which can support human life. Billions of people live here and each person's actions have an impact on our world.

Crisis on Planet Earth

The growth in population is threatening our future, and 1 billion people are not getting enough to eat. Every 20 minutes, the world adds another 3,500 human lives, but it loses one or more entire species of animal or plant life – at least 27,000 species per year.

- Our major energy source is oil. Once we have used it there will not be any more. The current known supply will last about 20 years.

- Seventy per cent of all developing world families depend upon wood for their energy. Trees are disappearing fast. In the last ten years, 1,554,000 square kilometres of forest have been cut down. Forests are the 'lungs of the planet' because they turn carbon dioxide into oxygen. Twenty-five years ago trees covered the Himalayan slopes. Today those trees are gone and farmers have cut down the underbrush because the growth in population has meant that they are desperate to grow crops. So

precious topsoil has been washed away by the rain and the water and topsoil has settled in India, flooding a huge area. The flooding continues into Bangladesh and brings disaster to this low-lying country.

We can't carry on polluting the air, land and water with substances which affect our health and which are changing our climate. We are producing more and more waste, losing important species, and using up our natural resources such as freshwater, fuels and minerals.

How can we reduce this ever-increasing pressure on our planet? Action is needed on a global scale to find alternative **renewable**, non-polluting sources of energy. For example the use of wind, solar, hydro-electric or wave power. We must learn to live and act in a way that is *sustainable* (can carry on indefinitely).

If not, future generations will suffer from our selfishness.

Agenda 21

In 1992 the United Nations called a meeting in Rio de Janeiro to discuss new ways of meeting the needs of the world. This was followed up by the Johannesburg Earth Summit in 2002. At these Earth Summits, world leaders discussed how people locally and globally could meet the needs of people in a sustainable way.

Sustainable development means that we provide for people in a way that:

- Looks after the environment.
- Involves everyone in the decisions about our future.
- Is fair to everyone.
- Takes into account the needs of future generations.

Governments pledged to try to do all four of these things to improve the quality of life for our world, our future and us.

▲ A mountain of waste.

At Rio, the world leaders agreed to a global action plan called 'Agenda 21'. This sets out everything that has to be done to promote sustainable development at local, national and international levels.

Local Agenda 21

Local Agenda 21 Strategies are 'local actions for the twenty-first century'. Each local council agrees them with their communities. They are a plan of how they are going to meet local needs in a sustainable way.

▲ Walking bus schemes.

DOVER DISTRICT COUNCIL

This council's Agenda 21 Strategy has led to:

1 Energy-saving schemes. Their council houses now have:

- double-glazed windows
- new energy-efficient boilers
- more loft insulation.

2 Reduction in pollution and traffic:

- incentives for car sharing
- more public transport
- better facilities for cyclists
- cash incentives for people who do not drive to work
- the walking school bus schemes. This is like an ordinary bus, with stops and a regular route and timetable. There is one major difference; everyone walks. Parents lead and follow the 'bus' to make sure the children are safe, and children join along the route.

3 Recycling:

- 15,000 pieces of furniture recycled each year by six paid employees and some volunteer helpers.
- Bicycles and electrical goods repaired.
- Unused paint recycled.

4 Community:

- The Friendship Project has been set up to help people of other nationalities and cultures settle in the area. Local children and asylum seekers have made kites with messages of hope for a peaceful future.

GLOSSARY

Asylum seekers: People who have left their own countries and applied to live here because their governments have persecuted them.

Renewable: Energy sources that don't run out.

Sustainable development: Development that doesn't harm the planet.

? Questions

1 Explain what is meant by sustainable development.
2 What does Agenda 21 set out to do?
3 Research the Local Agenda 21 Strategy in your area. (Ask your local council to explain it.)

Making a Difference

The human race is in great danger. Why?

- We have used up many of the earth's resources.
- We have damaged the **ozone layer**, which protects all life on earth from dangerous ultraviolet rays.
- We have polluted the air, water and land with poisons, pesticides and gases which cause global warming.
- We have created nuclear bombs and other weapons of mass destruction.
- Our world's population is growing too fast.
- We have allowed the gap between the very rich and the very poor to grow and grow.
- We have allowed many people to become very resentful, which may be shown in the spread of terrorism.

Thinking globally, acting locally

If we are going to get out of this mess this is what we must do.

Every area needs to take action towards sustainable development.

Every decision taken should consider the impact on our environment **and** the impact on other people's environment.

Examples of Agenda 21

In Britain – Yorkshire councils must not allow new factories if their air pollution would create acid rain in Sweden.

In West Africa – cocoa must now be grown in a sustainable way (e.g. a canopy of other trees must be introduced to protect the forest).

▲ Cocoa pods.

In Zimbabwe the wildlife and its habitat must be managed in a sustainable way. The Campfire Programme:

- Lets a limited number of tourists hunt wild animals.

▲ Wildlife in Zimbabwe.

- Lets local people sell a limited amount of natural products such as crocodile eggs.
- Trains local people as tourist guides and encourages tourism that doesn't harm the habitat by over-development.
- Lets local people catch live animals and sell them to Game Reserves if they are plentiful.
- Lets local people hunt and sell the meat if the animals are not endangered.

Campfire is a success because local people make money out of conserving the wildlife. Before this they were tempted to poach the animals.

What Can You Do?

'Every little helps'. Do you think it is your responsibility to help?

Which of the following suggestions do you think is a good idea a) for most people b) for yourself?

GLOSSARY

Global warming: When more carbon dioxide causes the seas to warm up, polar ice to melt and the climate to change.

Ozone Layer: Layer in the atmosphere that protects us from dangerous ultraviolet rays.

Think Global, Act Local: Phrase from the Rio Conference that aimed to get local communities working together on environmental issues to make a global impact.

Third World: Another name for less developed countries (LDCs).

	most people?	myself?
• reduce family size by using family planning		
• adopt/sponsor a child in a poor country		
• raise money for a Third World charity		
• get involved in your local community		
• educate yourself about global issues		
• ride a bike/walk if possible		
• use public transport/avoid big cars that waste petrol		
• pick up rubbish/don't leave litter		
• plant trees/conserve green space		
• recycle goods/create compost		
• use solar power/wind power		
• vote for parties that campaign on these issues		
• join groups/parties that campaign on these issues		

? Questions

1 Write a leaflet to explain to people of your age the dangers to life on earth.
2 What could people like you do?
  Make a list of practical suggestions for students in your school to consider. Remember, **Think Global, Act Local**.

Sustainable Development and Local Agenda 21

What is Genetic Modification?

Working in the laboratory scientists take the genes from one species and add them to the genes of another. This introduces quite new characteristics to plants or animals.

GM Food

In June 2003 the Government encouraged everyone to get involved in the debate about GM food.

Some people think genetic modification is morally and practically wrong – it will cause many more problems by tinkering with nature itself.

Others say genetic modification can help feed the world and solve many serious health problems.

Read on and update yourself on the great debate.

Selective breeding is not new. Farmers and animal breeders have tried for years to improve crops and animals in this way. They have bred plants and animals by putting together those with the features they want e.g. large straight carrots.

GM 'Flavr Savr' tomatoes have been modified to make them ripen more slowly. They last longer on supermarket shelves.

Why GM Food?

GM companies say that there are many possible future benefits of GM foods.

Benefits for consumers?
• To increase world food supplies/feed the starving. If corn could be modified so that it grows with less water, crops could grow in the desert.
• GM seeds could produce bigger yields from the land. This could feed the growing population.

Benefits for health?
• Crops could be modified to add vitamins and minerals. Vitamin A in Golden Rice could prevent some cases of blindness.
• Crops could be modified to make medicines. Cheaply-produced antibiotics and vaccines would save lives.

Benefits for farmers/companies?
• Insect-resistant crops mean farmers wouldn't have to use pesticides.
• Weedkiller-resistant crops mean farmers can spray the whole field and so increase yields by killing all weeds.

The Risks of GM Food?

Environmental campaigners say that there are many problems in growing GM foods.

• GM crops contaminate other crops for miles around with their pollen. Even organic farmers can't prevent this. Wild plants and bees can be contaminated too.
• Wildlife such as insects and birds need weeds and insects on farmland to survive. GM crops would destroy wildlife.

▲ Crop spraying by plane.

- GM crops could transfer their properties to other plants such as weeds. This could produce super weeds which no weedkiller could kill.

- Although GM food seems healthy, so far there have been no human trials of its long-term effects (unlike when new medicines are produced).

- Big multinationals would control the seeds. They would create a monopoly. Bio-diversity would suffer. These companies aren't really interested in what poor African farmers need. They simply want profits.

- The USA has already invested heavily in GM crops. Its government is trying to force EU countries to accept them as well. It doesn't want these foods labelled. So people wouldn't know whether they are eating them or not.

The Media

GM goes way beyond selective breeding.

No-one can say for sure what will happen to human health or the environment. The media in Britain have used negative headlines to dramatise this idea.

▲ **Protestor destroying a GM crop.**

FRANKENSTEIN FOODS

STOP GM FOODS

Terminator Genes

GLOSSARY

Organic farmers: Grow organic crops that are not contaminated by pesticides, weedkillers or GM varieties.

Pesticides: Chemicals that kill insects.

Vaccines: Drugs that protect you from getting certain diseases.

? Questions

1 Which view best sums up your attitude to GM Foods?

'I want the Government to be very cautious. They shouldn't allow GM crops to be grown in Britain until much more research has been done. I don't trust the GM supporters to think about the long-term consequences.'

'I think GM is a great new development. It could really help solve the important issues facing the world. I believe the research shows the food is safe to eat. I trust the scientists to do their best to look after our interests. The environment lobby are worried over nothing.'

2 Do protestors have the right to damage GM crops and if so why?

3 Carry out a small survey to find out people's attitudes to GM Foods. (You could ask them question 1 above and record their answers.)

What Price Petrol?

KEY ISSUES

○ What are the real costs of oil?
○ What alternatives are there to using petrol and cars?

The Energy Crisis – Why is it a Problem?

We are using up fossil fuels, especially oil, fast. Once they are gone we won't have oil, petrol, aircraft fuel or natural gas. We will have to use renewable sources of energy.

The UK

Like other developed countries Britain uses a lot of oil. Many Britons think:

🗣 *'It's my right to use my car whenever I want, to go wherever I want.'*

🗣 *'Petrol should be cheap. The Government has no right to tax cars or fuel as much as this.'*

The Government says, *'Oil will run out. How can we stop people using so much? If we make petrol and diesel more expensive by adding fuel duty and VAT, people will think twice about using their cars for every journey. The oil will last longer. The roads won't be so congested. We won't have to build new roads on farmland. Air pollution and asthma will decrease.'*

In the long run people can see that car use may have to decrease (or run on alternative fuels).

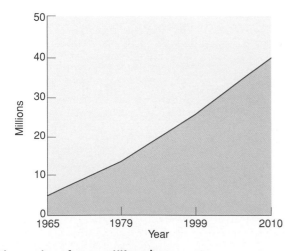

▲ The number of cars on UK roads.

In the short run people don't want to give up the convenience of their petrol-driven cars.

For every £50 worth of petrol £37 is tax (Fuel duty and VAT) This is more than in other EU countries. But Britain is an overcrowded island where traffic congestion is a big problem. Britain has promised to cut the amounts of **greenhouse gas** it produces. The government believes if petrol is cheap people will never reduce their car use until it is too late. But expensive petrol can annoy the public.

The 'Dump the Pump' campaign of 2000 started as a protest against petrol and diesel taxes when prices reached 84p per litre (see page 51). But the Government kept the tax the same. Prices went down anyway when world prices went down.

The Price of Crude Oil

Oil is traded on the world market. The biggest producer is Saudi Arabia, a member of OPEC. OPEC is a cartel (club) that controls how much oil its 11 members produce. They agree to sell it for between $22–28 a barrel. The higher price is used when there is a threat to supplies. In early 2003 the price of crude oil went up because of fears about a war in Iraq. By June 2003 the price of crude oil had fallen because the war was over.

The USA is not a member of OPEC and its oil companies are trying to open up oil and gasfields in non-OPEC countries e.g. in Africa. They want to become less dependent on oil from the Middle East. Petrol is very cheap in the USA. The average US citizen uses 22 barrels a year (more than any other country). The US Government has not signed up to the **Kyoto Agreement** to cut the amounts of greenhouse gases it produces.

Other Costs

The Exxon Valdez

Oil production often harms the environment. Spills in coastal waters are quite common. One of the worst was in 1989 when the Exxon Valdez tanker spilled over 11 million gallons of crude oil along the coast of Alaska.

- The **ecosystem** was destroyed. 20% of the oil was still there in 2002.
- Thousands of sea birds and otters were cleaned but thousands more died.
- The local fishing economy collapsed.

Political conflict
The oil trade produces billions of dollars. But local people don't always see the benefit. Nigeria has earned billions from its oil fields. But income for most Nigerians remains very low. Some Nigerians have grown very rich. This inequality harms stability.

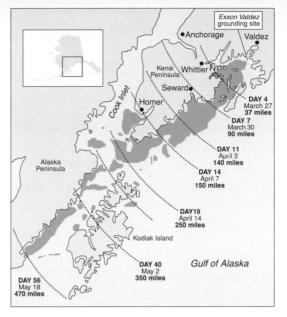

▲ This map shows the extent of the Exxon Valdez oil spill.

GLOSSARY

Ecosystem: System in which plants, fish, birds, mammals etc live and depend on each other.

Greenhouse gases: Carbon dioxide and other gases produced by burning fossil fuels that produce global warming.

Kyoto Agreement: International agreement to reduce the amount of greenhouse gases produced.

? **Question**

There are a number of possible solutions to reduce the use of fossil fuels. These include:

- Better public transport: trams, buses, trains to get us where we want.
- Cooperative travel: car-sharing or rent a car by the hour so fewer of us own cars.
- Steep rises in petrol prices.
- Road-pricing, toll roads and congestion charging to put us off driving in city centres or in rush hour.
- Cars that run on old chip fat or on LPG (Liquid Petroleum Gas): the emissions are less harmful.
- Using hydro-electric, wind, tides and solar power to generate electricity (instead of oil or natural gas).
- Electric cars with batteries powered by solar power.
- Make buildings more energy-efficient.

Which do you think have the best chance for cutting our use of fossil fuels? Explain your answers.

Case Study

The Future Citizen

The Past

Do your grandparents or great-grandparents tell you about just how much change there has been in their lifetimes? Someone in their eighties might say:

- 🗣 *'We didn't have television. We made our own entertainment.'*
- 🗣 *'We had landlines but no mobile phones.'*
- 🗣 *'No computers then.'*
- 🗣 *'All office work was paper-based.'*
- 🗣 *'We used the train or bus. Few families had cars.'*
- 🗣 *'We walked or cycled a lot.'*
- 🗣 *'It cost to go to the doctor or the dentist.'*

- 🗣 *'We took a week at the seaside for our summer holiday.'*
- 🗣 *'No freezers or convenience food then.'*
- 🗣 *'No supermarkets then.'*

What do you think you will say has changed, when you are in your eighties?

Active or Passive?

This course has given you both knowledge and skills. You understand more about how the world works: about power, rights and responsibilities. You have studied some problems and conflicts facing us all in the years to come. You have practised negotiating, discussing and making decisions.

▲ Will the future see environmental crisis, war and robots to do the work?

What are you going to do now to improve the world for your grandchildren?

Will you be an active citizen – someone who fully participates in their democracy and helps make it a better society?

Or will you be a passive citizen – someone who does not participate or question what is going on, who sits back and lets others make the decisions in society, who may just vote every 4 or 5 years?

By 2080	likely?	unlikely?
• No school. You learn at home via ICT		
• Robots run factories		
• Many jobs involve caring for others		
• Elderly people carry on working into their seventies		
• You vote at home about all important issues		
• No **nation states**. International government more important – United States of Europe/Africa/Asia		
• United Nations has become the government of the world		
• No-one starves. Plenty of good food available		
• Poor countries have caught up with rich countries		
• Racism is a thing of the past		
• The disadvantaged gain equal opportunities		
• Multinationals own and control everything		
• No more war or terrorism. Conflicts settled in other ways		
• Clean air and water for all		
• Pleasant landscape and cities for all		
• Crime reduced or solved		
• More leisure		
• More community spirit		

Remember – active citizens will keep themselves informed about these issues and make up their own minds. They will understand their own rights and take their responsibilities seriously. They will keep asking questions of those in power and insist their views are listened to. They will demand that those in power are **accountable** to those that put them there.

It is up to all of us to create the future we want to see.

The Future?

Maybe there will be even more change in your lifetime. Think about the citizenship issues you have studied. How will it be in 2080?

GLOSSARY

Accountable: In a democracy, leaders should be accountable to the people who put them there by explaining what they do and taking account of public opinion.

Nation State: When a nation has its own independent government e.g. France.

? Questions

1 Say what you think will happen by 2080 by saying whether the outcome is likely or unlikely and why.
2 Which of these outcomes would you like to see happen?

Examination Preparation

To pass the the AQA GCSE Citizenship (short course) you must:

- Answer questions in a 1½ hour written examination worth 60% of the marks.
- Complete coursework worth 40% of the marks.

The Question Paper has Four Sections:

Section A has 15 short-answer questions. Each question is worth 2 marks. The questions are about:

- Topic 1 – School and Work and Local Community
- Topic 2 – National and European Citizenship
- Topic 3 – Global Citizenship

You should revise all your notes carefully.

You will get 1 mark for an answer that is partly right. You will get 2 marks for a correct answer. 2–3 lines are available to write each answer.

Section B contains a stimulus (writing/ picture/table etc.) that you should read carefully. The stimulus could be about any part of the course.

You must answer one question which is usually divided into 3 parts.

Part a) is short. You answer it by reading the stimulus carefully.

Part b) is longer and worth more marks. To answer it fully you will need to use the stimulus and your own knowledge.

Part c) requires the longest and most detailed answer. You will be given more space for this question because it offers the most marks. Use the space as a guide for the amount you need to write.

In parts b) and c) you may be asked for your own opinion on the issue. Always back up your opinion with evidence from your studies or from your understanding of the news.

Make sure your answers are relevant and detailed. You can include real life situations/ experiences to support your answer.

Section B is worth 30 marks.

Section C will ask questions about a practical citizenship activity that you have done.

You can write about your coursework if you wish.

You will need to outline what the activity was.

Then you will be asked to explain what you have learned about citizenship from doing this activity.

For example:

- What did you learn from the planning stage?
- What was your involvement and contribution?
- What were the views, opinions and contributions of others?
- Was the activity successful?
- What lessons did you learn about citizenship?
- How would you do it differently next time? Why?

Remember your activity does not have to have been a complete success. You will gain good marks if you can describe what you learned from any problems.

Section C is worth 30 marks.

It would be very helpful to keep a copy of your coursework and read over it again before the examination.

In **Section D** you have a choice of three questions. You answer **one** question. It is worth 30 marks.

This question requires a short essay answer.

The three questions to choose from will cover the three themes of citizenship.

- Theme 1 – Rights and Responsibilities
- Theme 2 – Decision Making, Power and Authority
- Theme 3 – Participation in Citizenship Activities

Local, national and European, and global aspects will be covered.

Each question will suggest bullet points to help you to focus your answer on the task set. These prompts will help you with the structure of your essay. But you do not have to use them. You will not be penalized if you do not use the framework.

6 additional marks are available for spelling, punctuation and grammar.

Examples of the Type of Questions in Section A

Sample question A1
Name **two** ways you can participate in the electoral system when you are 21 years old. (2 marks)

- Vote at a recognised polling station. (would give you 1 mark)
- Stand for election as a candidate. (would give you 1 mark)
- Become an election agent. (would give you 1 mark)

Maximum 2 marks.

Sample question A2
What is meant by a 'multicultural society?' (2 marks)

A multicultural society includes people from a variety of cultures. People from different nations and ethnic backgrounds live together. (would give you 2 marks)

1 mark would be awarded if only 'cultures', 'variety of nations' or 'ethnic backgrounds' was given.

Sample question A3
What does CRE stand for? (2 marks)

Commission for Racial Equality. (would give you 2 marks)

An almost correct answer would give you 1 mark.

Examples of the Type of Questions in Section B
You may be given source material like this:

The Weekly News

The local Health Trust announced today that the Accident and Emergency unit at the Teemouth hospital will close in three months. The unit will be transferred to a larger hospital in the neighbouring town of Exton, some 15 miles away.

Local Council Leader Jean Smith said that the council would fight to keep the unit open.

Local MP Heather George, speaking from London, declared that she intended to join the fight to keep the Accident and Emergency unit open.

Sample question B1
Outline the nature of the issue affecting the community.

Sample question B2
Who else other than the local council and the MP could be involved in campaigning to keep the unit open?

Sample question B3
What methods could a campaign group use to persuade the Health Trust to change its mind and which are likely to be the most successful?

Examination Preparation

Examples of the Type of Questions in Section C

The questions in Section C refer to the practical citizenship activity in which you have been involved. Keep a copy of your final report and re-read it before your examination to refresh your memory of:

- The activity undertaken.
- The planning stages.
- The involvement of yourself and others.
- The final evaluation of the citizenship activity.

The response to the question does not have to be based upon your submitted coursework task. It could be based upon any citizenship activity you have done. You will be asked to explain what you have learned about citizenship from doing this activity.

Remember your activity does not have to have been a complete success. You will gain good marks if you can describe what you learned from any problems.

You will be asked to briefly outline what the activity was.

Sample question C1
Outline the planning that took place before the activity began. (5 marks)

Answer: What did you plan to do originally? What planning did other people do? A step-by-step plan of what you intended to do would be an ideal answer. Include:

- the preparation you did
- the strategies you used (e.g. research, group meetings)
- the aims and objectives you set yourself.

This would be worth full marks.

Sample question C2
Following the outline planning stage, describe your own contribution. (5 marks)

Answer: Include in detail:

- what you did and the contribution you made to the activity
- the strengths and weaknesses of your contribution.

Sample question C3
Describe the contribution made by other people associated with your citizenship activity and compare their contribution with your contribution. (10 marks)

Answer: Include:
- Details of what your peer group did.
- The contribution of older people (e.g. school staff).
- In what way(s) people gained from the activity.
- Compare, contrast and evaluate the contribution of other people.
- Analyse their strengths and weaknesses.

Sample question C4
How successful was the activity? What lessons were learned about the citizenship issue? What improvements could be made for the future? (15 marks)

Answer:
Level 1 (the first rung on the ladder) – you give a very short account of the activity with few clear points about its success. (1–3 marks)

Level 2 (second rung of the ladder) – you add an outline of the activities' success at a basic level. You include some of the lessons learned. (4–6 marks)

At Level 3 (having already achieved Level 2) you develop the lessons learned and the improvements that could be made in the future. You organise your answer to answer the question clearly. (7–9 marks)

At Level 4 your account analyses how successful the activity was. It is logically presented and supported by evidence. You explain how it could be improved by changing the planning or the carrying out of the activity. (10–12 marks)

At Level 5, to obtain the highest level and gain the full marks available, your response should give a full and detailed description of the lessons learned and the improvements that could be made. The points made should be logical and fully supported by the evidence given. The planning is linked to the progress made. Improvements suggested follow on from the experiences gained and evaluations made. Suggested improvements are practical and would fit the purposes of the task.

Examples of the Type of Questions in Section D

Each topic could have a local focus or a national and European focus or a global focus.

Sample question D1
Rights and Responsibilities.

Do you agree with the balance of rights and responsibilities in schools? (30 marks)

- Explain what you mean by the terms rights and responsibilities.
- How do parents, teachers and students have different rights and responsibilities?
- Discuss examples: attendance, behaviour, school rules, learning, bullying, homework.
- Give examples of what happens if there is a problem.
- Does the Human Rights Act affect rights and responsibilities in schools?
- In conclusion explain your own opinion on this issue.

Sample question D2
Decision Making, Power and Authority

'The electoral system for general elections in this country is fair.' Do you agree that the First Past the Post System works well for Britain? (30 marks)

- How does the system work at present?
- What are the advantages?
- What are the disadvantages?
- Would alternative systems be any better?
- In conclusion do you agree with the opening statement? Explain your own opinions on this issue.

Sample question D3
Participation in Citizenship Activities

'There's no point giving to Third World charities. The problems are so huge it won't make any difference.' Why do many people support development charities and voluntary groups? (30 marks)

- What do the different charities and groups aim to do?
- How does this small scale aid benefit Third World countries?
- How might it benefit people here who get involved?
- How is this kind of aid different from official government aid?
- Describe how you think giving to charity can make a difference.
- In conclusion what is your opinion regarding the opening statement.

> Remember – the bullet points are offered with each question to give you some help. You do not need to follow this guidance; you can offer your own structure and approach to answer the question.

How to Gain Full Marks

The questions in Section D will be marked on 6 Levels of response. Level 1 is a very basic response, while Level 6 will only be achieved by a very detailed account that fully answers the questions.

The responses for the questions above are marked as follows for each level:

Examination Preparation

- Level 1 answer – contains one or two points that are relevant. A poor descriptive account is given. (1–5 marks)
- Level 2 answer – a partial answer that contains several relevant points but is largely descriptive. (6–10 marks)
- Level 3 answer – most of the main points are covered in a structured way. Some points are fully developed, many are not. Some examples are given. Limited evaluations and conclusions are given. (11–15 marks)
- Level 4 answer – covers all the main points of the question. The response has a clear structure and includes examples. Some evaluation is given. (16–20 marks)
- Level 5/6 answers – a logical structured account is offered, covering all the main points which are supported by examples and evidence. Sound evaluation and clear conclusions are given in an integrated way. (Level 5 11–25 marks; Level 6 26–30 marks)

Coursework Guidance

KEY ISSUES

- Select an activity that you really wish to participate in and get fully involved with.
- Make sure it really is a citizenship issue.
- Be an active citizen taking real responsibility to learn about society and help others.
- Plan what you intend to do carefully.
- Write a report based on your activity.

A Challenge or an Opportunity?

Coursework is an essential part of the GCSE Citizenship (short course) examination. You will have to produce one piece of coursework of approximately 2000 words in length.

Coursework will count for 40 per cent of the total marks for the whole course.

Introduction

Your coursework must relate to your active participation within your school or the wider community. At this stage the more active your involvement the better. Desk-bound research will not be enough, although you may need to do some research to help produce a well-rounded piece of original work. You will need to give careful thought to the activity before, during and after its completion to make sure that you are able to demonstrate:

- Skills of active participation.
- Responsible action.

- Gaining knowledge and understanding relevant to citizenship.

A written report is required and you can write your report stage by stage as you undertake the activity. The final evaluation and conclusions should be written towards the end of the course. This will give you the opportunity to reflect on your work. Further ideas and examples are given on the next page.

Report Format

As you become actively involved and research your coursework, you may obtain and process a range of data, evidence and information. This may include:

- Questionnaire results.
- A case study.
- Survey findings.
- Interviews.
- Records of debates or speeches.
- Information from books/newspapers/internet.
- Letters that you have written/e-mails you have sent.
- Records of visits that you have made.

Above all, you must become actively involved and participate as a responsible citizen.

> Collect ideas → Start thinking → Start planning

Stage 1 – The Plan

- Outline what your citizenship activity is about and how it relates to this Citizenship Studies course.
- Write a brief introduction and discuss this with your teachers. Can you justify the activity?
- Is the activity school based or based in the wider community? Will you do it alone, in a group or in a combination of the two?
- Now list what you think you need to do in order to complete the coursework.

- Check with your teacher, discuss a structure and begin to develop an Action Plan.

Remember:

1 To list the various stages.
2 To list the intended outcomes.
3 To list what practical things you and others will need to do.
4 To think about how much time you will give to the activity.

Careful planning is the key at this stage.

Stage 2 – The Activity

You will need to write up an account of the citizenship activity – so keep all your rough notes. Keep a diary of what you do or plan to do:

- Indicate what, when, where and how you become involved.
- Say what you actually did.
- Say what other people your age, younger and older than you, did.
- Explain what roles and relationships you and others had.
- Indicate the rights and responsibilities you and others had.
- Show what research you did and why.
- Note what information was easy to obtain, who gave it to you and what was useful (be selective).
- Write it up; give your opinions, draw conclusions from what you have learned.
- Do not undersell yourself – if you were fully involved in the citizenship activity, say so!
- Say whether it was a five-day activity, as in Work Experience, or 30 minutes every day for a term or once a week.
- Say if it was a fund-raising event that involves you at various times of the day, evening or at weekends.

> HAS THAT MADE YOU THINK?

Stage 3 – The Evaluation

After the activity is undertaken you need to write it up, including the Planning Stage and the Activity Stage. The Evaluation Stage is last, but it is still very important.

You will need to draw together your opinions and conclusions, clearly stating:

- Your role, your views, your experience and the contribution you have made.
- The roles, views, experience and contributions of other people involved in the citizenship activity.
- Opinions and conclusions, reflections on the activity, its value to others, the planning and strategies you adopted (did they help you to achieve the initial aim?).
- What you learned, and what you and others gained from undertaking the activity.
- What changes you would recommend that would have 'improved' the activity.

> **Reminder** – the word limit is 2000 words – you may need to re-draft and use an appendix if your report is too long.

Resources List

Your activity may have involved gathering information from a variety of sources. All the resources you have used should be written on the resources list, which should be attached to your coursework report. Include useful website addresses.

Ideas for Coursework

The practical citizenship activity may be selected from within the subject content of this book.

- Topic 1. It may be school based, work based or based within the local community
- Topic 2. It could be based on national and European citizenship issues or criminal and civil law.

- Topic 3. It could be based on global issues. Think of global issues and how you could act locally to improve the quality of life for others.

The most important thing is that you must enjoy, value and be actively involved in the activity. The most important decision you will make is the first one! Choose the activity you really want to do. Negotiate this with your teachers.

Ideas for your Coursework Task

After talking to your teacher, you may decide to base your activity within school and to go it alone or work with other pupils (a whole-class activity is a possibility). Or you may decide to work in an active way in the wider community outside school. Look again at the work you have undertaken from this book and consider the following ideas. Then discuss the advantages and disadvantages of them before finally deciding on your active citizenship activity.

Topic 1: Local/Community Ideas

- Consider exploring the roles and responsibilities of employees and employers within your work experience placement/How does the company relate to the local, national and global economy?
- Consider how you could bring about change in your community. Perhaps you could help involve young people in sport, help regenerate a local problem area or get involved in activities which improve community understanding/race relations within your area.
- Work on a reading programme with younger students each week to improve their learning/set up a joint youth club activity with students with a disability.

Topic 2: National/European Ideas

- Think about a topical national or European issue, and investigate ways that you can get involved at a local level (e.g. it could be a political or environmental issue).

- Participate in a national organization that operates locally (e.g. Child Line) or organize a local activity and be part of a national event (e.g. Red Nose Day).

- Organize a mock election or local debating society.

- A national event is often reported differently by different sections of the media – you could canvass public opinion locally and report your findings.

- Think about school rules and how they might be changed for the better, e.g. can you influence a reduction in graffiti in school?

Topic 3: Global Ideas

- Does your school have contacts abroad? Can you take part in a cultural exchange or work abroad in your holidays helping on a community project?

- Help to organise a visiting speaker to address your group on a global issue.

- Get involved in a global environmental issue at a local level, e.g. recycling or reducing pollution.

- Make contact with refugee groups or human rights groups such as Amnesty. See how they campaign and get involved.

How Will the Coursework Be Assessed?

When undertaking your coursework it is useful to know how it will be assessed. It helps you to plan ahead and to pick up maximum marks as you go along. Remember these key points.

Your work will be assessed on the following:

- How well you plan your citizenship activity.

- How well you carry out the activity and how actively involved you are.

- Your knowledge and understanding of the citizenship activity.

- How well you obtain and explain the information you collect.

- How well you express your opinions and draw conclusions.

- How well you evaluate your work.

Marks Will Be Awarded for

Stage 1 – Planning

Plan carefully:

- Is the task clearly based upon the specification?

- Do you show a 'real' sense of purpose?

- How does the activity have a value to other people?

- Have you clearly thought through what needs to be done?

- Do you need to undertake any additional research?

The key is to plan carefully and to consider any problems you may meet. Remember that you have a limited amount of time to complete the coursework.

Stage 2 – The Activity (Part 1)

(I) Knowledge and understanding:

- Can you clearly show the knowledge and understanding that you have gained?

- Can you display an understanding and insight into the roles, relationships and rights of everyone involved in the activity, including your own, those of others who have helped you and the people who have benefited from the activity?

The key is how much knowledge and understanding you have gained from the activity itself, and from researching the wider issues of the activity.

Stage 2 – The Activity (Part 2)

(II) Explanation and interpretation of the evidence collected:

- You must gather, summarise and present a wide range of information and data, and present it effectively in your written report.

- You may offer some background research.

- You need to give opinions and draw conclusions based on the above.

- Make sure you keep a diary of everything you do.

The key is how you use the data you have collected, how it is summarized and presented.

Stage 3 – Evaluation

You must:

- Show active practical involvement over a period of time (the more active, the better!).
- Evaluate the good and bad points of the project, your Action Plan, the strategies used and the lessons learnt.
- Recognize your and others' views, experiences and contributions to the citizenship activity.
- Reflect on the value and success of the activity, the lessons you have learned/ achieved and the benefit gained by others (say what changes you would suggest).

The key is to evaluate what you did, what others did, what was achieved and what lessons were learned and what could have been improved.

Finally, remember the quality of written communication is also assessed, so redraft your report to write in a clear style, and check that spelling, punctuation and grammar are accurate.

Now it is Your Turn

In your groups, begin to discuss the ideas offered. Select one or two activities that interest you and think about the following points:

1 Give the activity a title and a very brief description of what it is and how it might develop.
2 Consider the resources you may need to get started.
3 How do you plan to use your time?
4 What personal skills will you need?
5 How will you gather the information you require?
6 How will you sort through the material and decide what is best to use in your final report?
7 What opinions and conclusions will you be able to draw from the activity?
8 How might it be improved?

Remember as you write up your report it has to have a structure to gain marks. Your coursework is worth 40 per cent of the final mark!

LAST MINUTE REMINDERS:

Remember you must:

- Plan.
- Give an account of your activity.
- Evaluate the activity.
- Produce a Resources List.

Glossary Index